Definit

MW01073733

Defined King James Bible

Extracted from the *DKJB* by Dr. Jung and his helpers in South Korea
With Additions and Enhancements by the original author of the definitions,
D. A. Waite, Jr. (M.A., M.L.A.)

4,114 Total Entries:

(294 Arc, 94 Obs, 32 Rare, 4 Poetic, 9 Dialec, 236 Gk, 86 Heb)

---

a testimony ~ i.e. an opportunity to testify or witness

a space ~ for a time

a ~ i.e. as a

abase ~ humble, humiliate; *Arc* lower, cast down

abased ~ humbled, humiliated; *Arc* lowered, cast down

abasing ~ humbling, humiliating; *Arc* lowering

abated ~ reduced in amount, degree, or force: diminished, weakened, deducted

abhor ~ hate, detest

abhorred ~ hated, detested

abhorrest ~ abhor: hate, detest

abhorreth ~ abhors ~ 5

abide after ~ remains according to

abide ~ remain, live, *Arc* stay; *Gk* wait for

abideth ~ abideth: remains, lives, continues as

abiding ~ remaining, continuing

abjects ~ miserable, wretched, degraded, lowly (ones)

abode ~ place where one lives or stays: home, residence, dwelling place

abode ~ past tense of abide: remained; stood fast; went on being; *Arc* stayed, resided (in or at)

abodest ~abode: past tense of abide: remained, stayed, dwelt

abomination ~ thing vile, disgusting, hateful, detestable, or loathsome

abominations ~ disgusting, hateful, detestable, loathsome things

abound ~ overflow abundantly

abounded ~ *Gk* overflowed, excelled

aboundeth ~abounds: overflows greatly

abounding ~ greatly or abundantly overflowing

abounds ~ overflows abundantly

about the space of ~ i.e. for about

about ~ all around; around

above that ~ beyond what

above ~ more than, beyond, over

above measure ~ i.e. beyond counting

abroad ~ i.e. widely

abroad ~ outside; far and wide; outdoors; *Gk* into view

abstinence ~ *Gk* abstinence from food

abundant ~ well-supplied, plentiful; great, rich

acceptation ~ agreement; *Arc* acceptance

acceptest ~ accept ~ 1

accepteth ~ accepts ~ 4

accomplished ~ completed

accord ~ in agreement, harmony; *Gk* one-minded; choice

accord ~ *Gk* united in spirit or harmonious

account ~ consider
account ~ an answer or explanation
    for conduct
accounted ~ counted, considered;
    credited
accounting ~ taking into account,
    considering
accursed ~ under a curse; deserving
    to be cursed; abominable
accuseth ~ accuses ~ 1
acknowledgeth ~ acknowledges ~ 1
acquaintance ~ persons known, but
    not intimately
activity ~ *Heb* ability, efficiency
adamant ~ in ancient times, a hard
    stone or substance that was
    supposedly unbreakable
addeth ~ adds ~ 4
addicted ~ devoted; dedicated
adjure ~ command or charge
    solemnly, often under oath or
    penalty
adjured ~ commanded or charged
    solemnly, often under oath or
    penalty
admiration ~ *Arc* astonishment,
    surprise, wonder
admired in ~ *Arc* marveled at by
admonish ~ warn, encourage
admonished ~ warned, encouraged
admonition ~ warning, mild rebuke,
    reproof
ado ~ trouble, fuss; uproar
adorn ~ embellish, decorate, beautify
adorned ~ decorated, beautified
adorneth ~ adorns: decorates,
    beautifies ~ 1
adorning ~ beautification, decoration
adria ~ the Adriatic sea
advantage ~ profit, usefulness
advantaged ~ profited, benefited

advantageth it me ~ i.e. profit or
    benefit is it to me
advantageth ~ advantages: profits,
    benefits ~ 1
adventure ~ venture, dare; *Obs* dare
    to go
adventured ~ risked
adversaries ~ opponents, enemies
adversary ~ enemy, opponent
advertise ~ tell, inform
advisement ~ careful consideration;
    counsel, advice
afar off ~ *Arc* at or from a distance;
    Gk from a distance
affairs ~ concerns
affect ~ seek, pursue, have affection
    for
affected ~ sought, pursued
affecteth ~ affects ~ 1
affinity ~ a relationship formed by
    marriage
affirm ~ firmly declare, confirm
afflict ~ mistreat
afflictest ~ afflict ~ 1
affording ~ furnishing, providing,
    giving, yielding
affright ~ *Arc* frighten, terrify
affrighted ~ *Arc* frightened, terrified
afoot ~ on foot
afore ~ *Dialect* before
afore ~ before
aforehand ~ beforehand
aforetime ~ *Arc* formerly, in times
    past
after ~ afterwards, in connection with
    (Gk); i.e. afterwards, later; *Gk*
    according to
against ~ in preparation for; until; by
    the time of; by the time that;
    opposite to; next to; *Arc*
    before; *Gk* in
agone ~ long before; *Arc* ago, past

agreeth ~ agrees: matches, harmonizes

ague ~ a fever, usually malarial, marked by regularly re-curring chills

ailed ~ troubled, bothered

aileth ~ ails: bothers, troubles, causes pain or distress

albeit ~ although, even though

algum ~ tree from Lebanon

alienated ~ made foreign, estranged, excluded

aliens ~ foreigners

all to brake ~ wholly or completely broke i.e. crushed

all hail ~*Arc* greetings; *Gk* rejoice

alleging ~ declaring

allow ~ acknowledge; *Gk* know

allow ~ approve, applaud; admit, accept

alloweth ~ allows: accepts, approves

allure ~ entice, tempt with a lure

almost ~ very nearly, but not completely; *Gk* with a little

alms ~ Money or goods given as charity to the poor; *Obs* deeds of mercy

almsdeeds ~ Money or goods given as charity to the poor; *Obs* deeds of mercy

aloof ~ at a distance

altereth ~alters: changes

altogether ~ entirely, totally

alway ~ *Arc* of always

amazed ~ *Obs* perplexed, alarmed, stunned

amazement ~ *Arc* fear-paralysis

ambassage ~ group of men sent out on a mission; a delegation

ambushment ~ ambush

ambushments ~ ambushes: persons hiding for attack

amend ~ improve; correct, emend, reform

amerce ~ punish by imposing an arbitrarily determined fine; punish generally

amiable ~ *Obs* lovely or lovable

amiss ~ in a wrong way, wrongly, improperly, astray

amongst ~ among

an hungred ~ hungry

an hundredfold ~ a hundred times as much

an help ~ i.e. a helper

an hand breadth ~ a hand's width

an advocate ~ one who pleads our case

an eight ~ eight

an hungred ~ hungry ~ 9

anathema ~ thing or person accursed or greatly detested

angle ~ hook and line used for fishing

anguish ~ great suffering, agony, distress, grief

anise ~ plant used for spice and medicine: dill

anointedst ~ anointed ~ 1

anointest ~ anoint ~ 1

anon ~ *Arc* immediately, at once

another ~ *Gk* another (of the same kind)

answer ~ reasoned defense; *Gk* apologia

answeredst ~ answered ~ 2

answerest ~ answer ~ 6

answereth ~answers: corresponds

answering again ~ talking back

any wise ~ any way

any while ~ i.e. for a long time

any ways ~ in any way or manner

apace ~ swiftly; with speed; at a fast pace

apart ~ aside

apothecaries ~ pharmacists or druggists
apothecaries' ~ pharmacists' or druggists'
apothecary ~ pharmacist or druggist
apparel ~ clothing, garments, attire;
apparelled ~ clothed, attired
appeareth ~ appears ~ 10
appeaseth ~ appeases ~ 1
appertain ~ pertain, relate, have to do with
appertained ~ pertained, related, had to do with
appertaineth ~ appertains: pertains, relates, has to do with
appertains ~ pertains, relates, has to do with
appointeth ~ appoints ~ 1
apprehended ~ *Obs* seize(d)
approacheth ~ approaches ~ 1
approvest ~ approve ~ 1
approveth ~ approves ~ 1
apt ~ *Arc* prepared, ready; *Gk* skillful
aquaintance ~ acquaintances
are asleep ~ i.e. are dead
aright ~ correctly, rightly; in a right way
ariseth ~ arises ~ 11
ark ~ box, chest, coffer
armholes ~ armpits or arm openings in a garment
armour ~ armor ~ 24
armourbearer ~ armorbearer ~ 18
armoury ~ armory ~ 3
arms ~ weapons; *Heb* forces
array ~ finery, apparel; military order or battle formation
arrayed ~ richly, royally, finely, lavishly dressed or clothed; dressed in fine, showy attire; decked out; dressed up
art mindful of ~ *Gk* remember

art ~ *Arc* are
artificer ~ skilled craftsman; inventor
artificers ~ skilled craftsmen; inventors
artillery ~ *Arc* apparatus for hurling missiles; bow & arrows
arts ~ i.e. magic or sorcery
as ~ seeing that, since, because; to the extent that
ascend ~ go (up)
ascended up ~ went up
ascended ~ went or gone up
ascendeth ~ goes up
ascendeth ~ ascends ~ 2
ascending ~ going up
ascribe ~ attribute, assign, impute; impute
askest ~ ask ~ 3
asketh ~ asks ~ 11
asp ~ any of several venomous African, Asian, or European snakes including some vipers and cobras
asps ~ any of several venomous African, Asian, or European snakes including some vipers and cobras
ass ~ donkey, burro
assay ~ attempt, try
assayed ~ attempted, tried
assaying ~ attempting, trying
assent ~ consent, agreement
assented ~ consented, agreed
asses ~ donkeys, burros
assuredly gathering ~ definitely concluding
assuredly ~ certainly, confidently
asswage ~ assuage--relieve; make less intense or severe
asswaged ~ old spelling of assuaged--decreased, subsided, abated;

were made less intense or severe

astonied ~ *Obs* astonished: lit. "like a stone"

asunder ~ apart; into pieces or parts

at variance ~ put or place in conflict or disagreement; *Gk* cut into two parts, sever

at ~ near; to; i.e. out; i.e. in

at a venture ~ by mere chance, randomly

at enmity ~ having a strong, settled feeling of hatred

at even ~ *Arc* in the evening

at hand ~ i.e. near

at length ~ finally, after a long time

at strife ~ i.e. in conflict

at unawares ~ unintentionally, without knowing or being aware; unexpectedly, suddenly, by surprise

athirst ~ *Arc* thirsty

atonement ~ reconciliation; restoration to favor

attain to ~ reach

attained ~ achieved; arrived; *Gk* closely followed

attend upon ~ serve

attend ~ hear; *Arc* pay attention (to)

attendance ~ attention; service

attended to ~ *Arc* paid attention to, heard

attended ~ *Arc* paid attention

attending continually upon ~ *Gk* being steadfastly attentive unto

attent ~ attentive

augment ~ enlarge; increase

aul ~ *Arc* spelling of awl--pointed tool for making holes

austere ~ harsh, severe, or stern in look or manner

availeth ~ avails: has power to accomplish; is of use, help, or worth for; profits

avenge ~ inflict the Lord's deserved punishment; take revenge on behalf of

avenge not ~ do not take revenge on behalf of

avenge me of ~ inflict deserved, just punishment upon

avenged ~ inflicted punishment on behalf of

avenger ~ punisher

avengeth ~ avenges ~ 2

averse ~ turned away: unwilling, reluctant

avouched ~ openly acknowledged; asserted; affirmed

awakest ~ awake ~ 2

awaketh ~ awakes ~ 3

away with ~ tolerate, endure

axletrees ~ axles: shafts on which wheels rotate

babbler ~ producer of foolish, meaningless talk

backbiters ~ slanderers; those who speak maliciously about (an absent person)

backbiteth ~ backbites: slanders; speaks maliciously about (an absent person)

backbiting ~ slandering; speaking maliciously about (an absent person)

backbitings ~ slanderings; speakings maliciously about (an absent person)

bade ~ invited, asked, told; commanded (past tense of bid)

badest ~ bade> bid: told, asked, commanded

bag ~ money-bag

bakemeats ~ *Obs* pastries, pies; baked foods

baketh ~ bakes ~ 1

Balac ~ Balak ~ 1

balm ~ soothing ointment, salve

bands ~ things that bind, restraints: fetters, shackles, chains; *Heb* bonds; pangs; *Gk* ligaments

banquetings ~ carousings, drinking parties

baptizest ~ baptize ~ 1

baptizeth ~ baptizes ~ 2

barbarian ~ non-Greek, non-Roman; uncivilized, uncultured, crude, primitive

barbarians ~ non-Greeks, non-Romans; uncivilized, uncultured, crude, primitive ones

barbarous ~ non-Greek, non-Roman; uncivilized, uncultured, crude

bare ~ bore: carried, took up, lifted; gave; *Arc* of bore

barest ~ bear ~ 3

barked ~ stripped of all bark

barren ~ sterile, unable to conceive; empty

base ~ low(est), common, contemptible; *Obs* low or inferior in place or position

basest ~ lowest, most contemptible

bastard ~ illegitimate child

bastards ~ children born out of wedlock (illegitimately)

bath ~ Ancient *Heb* unit: 1 bath=6-10 gal

baths ~ Ancient *Heb* units: 1 bath=6-10 gal

battlement ~ parapet--a low protective wall or railing along the edge of a raised structure such as a roof or balcony

battlements ~ parapets--low protective walls or railings along the edge of a raised structure such as a roof or balcony

be no ~ are not

be mindful of ~ remember

be at charges ~ *Gk* incur expenses

bear long with them ~ puts up with them for a long time

bear ~ carry, sustain, support, lift; tolerate, put up with; *Gk* bear up under; endure; *Gk* wear, bear

bearest ~ bear ~ 5

beareth ~ bears: carries

bearing about ~ carrying around

bearing ~ carrying

beatest ~ beat ~ 2

beateth ~ beats ~ 1

became into ~ i.e. formed

became ~ was becoming to; was suitable or proper for

becamest ~ became ~ 2

beckoned ~ signaled; called or summoned by a silent gesture

beckoning ~ calling or summoning by a silent gesture as with a wave or nod; signaling

become ~ adorn: are right, fit, suitable, proper for

becometh us ~ is proper or fitting for us

becometh ~ becomes: suits, befits; adorns; is fitting to or proper for; is suitable to, worthy of, or appropriate for

bedstead ~ framework for supporting a mattress or bed

beeves ~ alternate plural of beef--a full-grown steer, bull, ox, or cow, especially one raised for meat

befall ~ happen (to)
befallen ~ happened (to)
befalleth ~ befalls: happens (to)
befell ~ happened or occurred (to)
beforetime ~ *Arc* formerly; at a time now past
begat ~ fathered, sired, procreated; produced
beget ~ father, sire, procreate; produce
begeteth ~ begets--fathers, sires, procreates; produces
begettest ~ beget: father, sire, procreate; produce
beggarly ~ inadequate; worthless; helpless; powerless
beginnest ~ begin ~ 1
begotten ~ fathered, sired, procreated; produced; generated
beguile ~ mislead or deprive by cheating or trickery; deceive; cheat, delude, trick
beguiled ~ deceived, cheated, deluded, tricked, misled
beguiling ~ deceiving, cheating, deluding, tricking, misleading
behaveth ~ behaves ~ 1
behaviour ~ behavior ~ 4
beheld ~ saw, observed, watched, looked at
behemoth ~ huge animal: perhaps an extinct dinosaur
behold ~ look at, see, observe, view closely, gaze upon; look upon; look! see!
beholdest ~behold: observe
beholdeth ~ beholds: looks at
beholding ~ seeing, watching
behoved ~ behooved: was necessary or proper for
being mindful of ~ remembering

belied ~ told lies about; misrepresented; contradicted; falsely portrayed
believest ~ believe ~ 8
believeth ~ believes ~ 45
belongest ~ belong ~ 1
belongeth ~ belongs ~ 20
bemoan ~ lament; mourn over; show grief or pity over
bemoaned ~ lamented; mourned over; showed grief or pity over
bemoaning ~ lamenting; mourning over; showing grief or pity over
bendeth ~ bends ~ 2
bent ~ determined, inclined
bereave ~ deprive or rob
bereaved ~ deprived, robbed
bereaveth ~ bereaves ~ 1
beseech ~ beg, entreat, implore; ask (someone) earnestly
beseeching ~ begging, entreating, imploring; asking earnestly
beset ~ encircle, surround; enclose; harass
beset ~ encircled, encompassed, surrounded; enclosed; harassed
beside ourselves ~ insane, crazy
beside ~ besides, in addition to
beside himself ~ insane, crazy
besieged ~ surrounded by an army (for a long time & cut off from supply)
besom ~ broom (made of twigs tied to a handle)
besought ~ begged, entreated, implored; asked (someone) earnestly
bestead ~ ill-treated, hard-pressed
bestir ~ stir-up, activate; rouse
bestow upon ~ give, present (as a gift or honor)

bestow ~ give, present, confer (as a gift or honor); *Arc* put, house, store

bestowed ~ given/gave, presented, conferred (as a gift or honor); *Arc* housed, put, stored, i.e. kept

bethink ~ *Arc* cause (oneself) to reflect on or consider remember; remind (oneself); recollect, recall

bethink themselves ~ *Arc* cause (oneself) to reflect on or consider remember; remind (oneself); recollect, recall

betimes ~ early, in good time; quickly; promptly, soon.

betrayest ~ betray ~ 1

betrayeth ~ betrays ~ 3

betroth ~ *Obs* promise to marry

betrothed ~ promised in marriage; engaged; *Obs* contracted to marry

bettered ~ improved, made better

betwixt ~ between, among

betwixt ~ between ~ 16

bewail ~ lament, mourn, wail over, express sorrow or unhappiness over

bewailed ~ lamented, mourned, wailed over; expressed sorrow or unhappiness over

bewaileth ~ bewails: laments, mourns, wails over; expresses sorrow or unhappiness over

bewitched ~ placed under his power by or as if by magic; cast a spell over; captivated completely; entranced

bewray ~ *Arc* divulge; reveal; betray

bewrayeth ~ bewrays: *Arc* divulges; reveals; betrays

bid you ~ i.e. tell you to

bid ~ ask, invite, tell; command; i.e. make

bidden ~ invited, asked, told (past tense of bid)

biddeth ~ bids: asks, invites, tells

bier ~ portable framework supporting a corpse or casket

bindeth ~ binds ~ 9

bishop ~ overseer

bishoprick ~ overseership; office or rank of an overseer

bishops ~ overseers

biteth ~ bites ~ 4

bittern ~ small bird similar to a heron

black ~ sad, dismal, gloomy; *Heb* dark, mournful

blackish ~ black-like

blains ~ skin swellings or sores; blisters; blotches; boils

blaspheme ~ speak of (God or a sacred entity) in an irreverent, impious manner; curse, revile; execrate

blasphemed ~ spoke(n) of (God or a sacred entity) in an irreverent, impious manner; cursed, reviled; execrated

blasphemer ~ one who speaks of (God or a sacred entity) in an irreverent, impious manner; one who curses, reviles, or execrates

blasphemers ~ ones who speak of (God or a sacred entity) in an irreverent, impious manner; ones who curse, revile, or execrate

blasphemest ~ speak irreverently, impiously

blasphemest ~ blaspheme ~ 1

blasphemeth ~ blasphemes: speaks of (God or a sacred entity) in an

irreverent, impious manner;
curses, reviles; execrates
blaspheming ~ cursing, reviling
blasting ~ any of several plant
diseases of diverse causes,
resulting in sudden death of
buds, flowers, foliage, or
young fruits; the withering
caused by atmospheric
conditions
blaze ~ proclaim, publish
blemish ~ deformity
blessest ~ bless ~ 3
blesseth ~ blesses ~ 8
blindeth ~ blinds ~ 1
blotted out ~ erased
blotteth ~ blots ~ 1
bloweth ~ blows ~ 4
blueness ~ Heb: bruise, stripe
boastest ~ boast ~ 1
boasteth ~ boasts ~ 4
boisterous ~ rough and stormy,
turbulent
bolled ~ budded; (boll=roundish seed
pod of a plant)
bolster ~ pillow, cushion; *Heb* head
place
bond ~ bond-slave; *Gk* doulos
bond ~ band, fetter, shackle; i.e.
bondage
bond ~ contract, covenant, binding
agreement; a duty or
agreement by which one is
bound; a promise
bondmaid ~ slave-girl
bondmaids ~ slavegirls
bondman ~ slave (male)
bondmen ~ slaves (male)
bonds ~ bands, chains, fetters,
shackles
bondservant ~ slave
bondservice ~ slavery

bondwoman ~ slave (female)
bondwomen ~ slaves (female)
bonnets ~ caps
booties ~ plunder
booty ~ plunder, loot
borne of ~ carried by
borne ~ tolerated, put up with;
carried, taken, lifted up; *Gk*
worn, born
borrow ~ ask
borrowed ~ asked
borroweth ~ borrows ~ 1
bosom ~ chest; i.e. robe-covered chest
area
bosses ~ knobs or projections
protruding from a flat surface
botch ~ boil, ulcer, tumor, or other
eruptive disease; swelling,
pimple, sore,
bound ~ compelled, obliged
bound ~ boundary, limit
bounds ~ boundaries, limits
bountifully ~ generously
bountifulness ~ generosity
bounty ~ generosity; gift freely given
bow ~ i.e. rainbow
bowels ~ interior of anything, esp. the
body: guts, intestines, innards;
Arc the seat of pity or the
gentler emotions: fig.
compassionate feelings or
tender emotions
boweth ~ bows ~ 3
bowing ~ curved, crooked
box ~ *Heb* vial, flask
box ~ evergreen like the boxwood
brakest ~ break> broke ~ 5
bramble ~ prickly, thorny shrub
brand ~ stick that is burning
brasen ~ brazen: like brass in color or
other qualities; brass=a
yellowish metal essentially an

alloy of copper and zinc: from an OE word meaning brass or bronze; *Heb* copper or bronze (a copper alloy)

bray ~ crush or pound into powder, as in a mortar; pulverize

bray ~ make the loud, harsh cry of a donkey

brayed ~ made the loud, harsh cry of a donkey

breach of promise ~ breaking of promise; *Heb* opposition

breach ~ break, crack, gap, broken place; breaking, bursting forth, outburst (of anger)

breaches ~ breaks, cracks, gaps, broken places or parts

breakest ~ break> broke ~ 1

breaketh ~ breaks ~ 17

breatheth ~ breathes ~ 1

breeches ~ garments that cover the breech or buttocks i.e. undergarments; trousers reaching to the knees

brethren ~ brothers

brickkiln ~ kiln (or furnace) for drying bricks

bridleth ~ bridles ~ 1

brigandine ~ armor; originally armor for a brigand (irregular soldier, robber, bandit)

brigandines ~ armor (plural); originally armor for a brigand (irregular soldier, robber, bandit)

brimstone ~ lit burn-stone--sulfur: burns with a blue flame & stifling odor, used in making black gun powder

bring forward on ~ *Gk* provide the necessities for

bringest ~ bring ~ 5

bringeth ~ brings ~ 79

brink ~ edge, bank

broided ~ braided, interwoven

broidered ~ embroidered, adorned with needlework

broughtest ~ brought ~ 13

bruit ~ *Arc* rumor, report, sound, noise; news; fame

brutish ~ beast-like: stupid, irrational; brutal, cruel; crude, uncivilized

buckler ~ small round shield held by a grip or worn on the arm; any protection or defense

bucklers ~ small, round arm-shields

buffet ~ strike with the fist or hand; punch, slap

buffeted ~ struck with the hand or fist: slapped; punched

buildedst ~ builded> ~ built ~ 1

buildeth ~ builds ~ 9

bullock ~ young bull, steer; male cattle raised for beef

bullocks ~ young bulls, steers; male cattle raised for beef

bulrush ~ marshland plant like the cattail or papyrus

bulrushes ~ marshland plants like the cattail or papyrus

bulwarks ~ defensive walls, earthworks

bunches ~ *Obs* humps

burneth ~ burns ~ 18

burnished ~ polished

busybodies ~ gossips, meddlers

busybody ~ gossip, meddler

butlership ~ office of butler

buyest ~ buy ~ 2

buyeth ~ buys ~ 3

by the space of ~ i.e. for; *Obs* for

by reason of ~ i.e. because; *Gk* through

by ~ in; nearby; *Gk* through

by an equality ~ out of fairness
by and by ~ immediately, at once
by occasion of ~ through
by reason ~ i.e. because
byword ~ object of scorn, ridicule, reproach or derision
calamities ~ great or deep troubles or miseries; disasters
calamity ~ great or deep trouble or misery; disaster
caldron ~ large kettle
caldrons ~ large kettles
call over ~ *Gk* name upon
calledst ~ called ~ 4
callest ~ call ~ 3
calleth ~ calls ~ 30
calve ~ give birth to a calf
calved ~ gave birth to a calf
calveth ~ calves: gives birth to a calf
camest ~ came ~ 28
can skill ~ *Obs* has/have skill
canker ~ anything that corrupts or gradually decays; gangrene, malignant growth, ulcer; rust; from L cancer
cankered ~ rusted, corrupted, decayed, eaten away
cankerworm ~ any of several larvae of geometrid moths harmful to fruit and shade trees, esp the spring cankerworm that feeds on fruit and foliage
canst ~ can ~ 51
carbuncle ~ *Arc* any of certain deep-red gems
carbuncles ~ *Arc* any of certain deep-red gems
care of ~ concern for
care ~ concern, anxiety, or worry
care ~ be concerned, worried, or anxious

careful ~ full of care, worry, or concern: anxious, worried, concerned
carefulness ~ anxiety, worry, concern
careless ~ worry-free; securely, safely
carelessly ~ in a worry-free manner
cares ~ worries, anxieties, concerns
carest ~ care ~ 3
careth ~ cares ~ 7
carnal ~ material; *Gk* fleshly
carnally ~ i.e. sexually
carriage ~ that which is carried: luggage, baggage
carriages ~ things that are carried: luggage, baggage
carriest ~ carry ~ 1
carrieth ~ carries ~ 3
carry tales ~ slander
cast lots ~ randomly make decisions using objects
cast out ~ *Gk* exposed
cast the same in his teeth ~ likewise taunted or mocked
cast their young ~ i.e. miscarried
cast their young ~ i.e. miscarry
cast up ~ construct by digging
cast forth ~ thrown out
cast clouts ~ cast-off or discarded pieces of cloth or rag often used as patches
cast angle ~ fish with a hook and line
cast a mount ~ build (*Obs*) a raised fortification
cast ~ *Gk* revolved, turned over
cast ~ threw; Brit vomited
cast ~ threw
cast ~ throw, fling, or hurl (with force or violence); drive; throw, i.e. spit
cast ~ thrown
cast ~ build, construct; form by pouring into mold

castaway ~ reject, discard

castedst ~ casted> ~ cast ~ 1

castest ~ cast ~ 3

casteth not her calf ~ delivers not her young prematurely

casteth ~ casts: throws, drops

casting up mounts ~ building (*Obs*) raised fortifications

casting ~ mold

casting ~ throwing, putting

catcheth ~ catches ~ 3

caul ~ membrane or fatty tissue surrounding an organ

cauls ~ close fitting caps or nets worn by women

causest ~ cause ~ 2

causeth ~ causes ~ 32

causeway ~ paved road, highway

cease to pray ~ i.e. stop begging, imploring, or beseeching

cease ~ stop

ceased to kiss ~ i.e. stopped kissing

ceased ~ stopped

ceaseth ~ ceases ~ 10

ceasing of ~ stopping by

ceasing ~ stopping; intermission

celestial ~ heavenly; pertaining to the sky or heavens; of heavenly origin or nature

censer ~ container in which incense is burned (a shortened form of ME encenser)

centurion ~ Roman commander of 100 soldiers

centurions ~ Roman commanders each in charge of 100 men

certain ~ certain (ones)

certain ~ fixed, definite

certified ~ assured, informed (with certainty)

certify ~ inform (with certainty); *Arc* assure

chafed ~ irritated, annoyed

challengeth ~ challenges ~ 1

chamber ~ room

chambering ~ *Arc* sexual indulgence or lewdness

chamberlain ~ originally, the bedchamber attendant of a ruler or lord; later, a ruler or lord's household manager, steward; *Heb* official, eunuch

chamberlains ~ originally, the bedchamber attendants of a ruler or lord; later, a ruler or lord's household managers, stewards; *Heb* officials, eunuchs

chambers ~ rooms

chamois ~ small mountain goat-antelope having straight horns with tips bent backwards; a soft leather made from the skin of such an animal

champaign ~ broad plain; flat, open country

chance ~ happen to be

chanceth ~ chances ~ 1

changest ~ change ~ 1

changeth ~ changes ~ 2

chapiter ~ top part (head or capital) of a column, pillar, or pilaster

chapiters ~ top parts (heads or capitals) of a column, pillar, or pilaster

chapmen ~ *Arc* peddlers, traders, merchants; men whose business is buying and selling

chapt ~ chapt=chapped: cracked open, split; roughened

charge ~ responsibility, duty; custody, care, supervision

charge ~ command, warn

charge ~ command, warning

chargeable ~ burdensome, a burden

charged ~ warned, commanded, ordered; entrusted; burdened
chargedst ~ charged ~ 1
charger ~ *Arc* platter; large, flat dish; something that carries a load (from charge: to load)
chargers ~ *Arc* platters; large, flat dishes; things that carry a load (from charge: to load)
charges ~ duties, responsibilities; expense
chargest ~ charge ~ 1
charging ~ warning, comanding
charitably ~ in a manner consistent with unselfish concern
charity ~ the love of God for humanity, or a love of one's fellow human beings; an act of goodwill or affection; the feeling of goodwill, benevolence; kindness or leniency in judging others; a voluntary giving of money or other help to those in need; money or help so given; an institution or other recipient of such help (In the KJV charity is always a translation of the Greek word agapA, a word that suggests unselfish, self-sacrificing concern.)
chaseth ~ chases ~ 1
chasten ~ correct by punishing: correct, punish
chastened ~ punished, beaten
chastenest ~ chasten ~ 1
chasteneth ~ chastens: correctively punishes: severely rebukes with words & chastises with blows
chastise ~ punish by beating
chastiseth ~ chastises ~ 1

check ~ any sudden stop or repulse (from the game of chess); *Obs* reproof, reprimand, rebuke, censure; *Heb* discipline, correction, chastening
cheereth ~ cheers ~ 1
cherisheth ~ cherishes ~ 2
cheweth ~ chews ~ 8
chide ~ loudly or passionately express anger, dissatisfaction, disappointment, disagreement, or discouragement: argue, quarrel, complain
chiding ~ loudly or passionately expressing anger, dissatisfaction, disappointment, disagreement, or discouragement: arguing, quarreling, complaining, contending
chief rooms ~ most important places (at table)
chief ~ *Gk* presidents
chief ~ main; greatest; i.e. leaders
chiefest ~ *Gk* first in rank or honor
chiefly ~ especially; mainly
chode ~ loudly or passionately expressed anger, dissatisfaction, disappointment, disagreement, or discouragement: argued, quarreled, complained
choler ~ anger, wrath, irascibility, ill-humor (Latin for bile, thought to be the source of anger and irritability)
choosest ~ choose ~ 2
chooseth ~ chooses ~ 3
church ~ assembly
churl ~ rude, coarse, surly, ill-bred person; boor; selfish or mean person; villain; *Heb* scoundrel, knave

churlish ~ rude, coarse, surly, ill-bred; boorish; selfish or mean; villainous; *Heb* hard, cruel, severe, stubborn

cieled ~ ceiled: covered or lined with plaster or thin boards (used of a room's ceiling or walls); *Heb* wainscoted, paneled

circuit ~ going around; circular path; orbit; i.e. a regular, circular route

circumspect ~ cautious, wary, careful; considerate; discreet, prudent; careful to consider all circumstances before acting, judging, or deciding;

circumspectly ~ cautiously, warily, carefully; considerately; discreetly, prudently; carefully considering all circumstances before acting, judging, or deciding;

cistern ~ container for catching rainwater

clamour ~ clamor: *Gk* loud demand or complaint

clappeth ~ claps ~ 1

clave ~ clung

clave ~ split

clean ~ completely

cleanseth ~ cleanses ~ 3

clear ~ pure, clean

clear ~ acquit; free; excuse

clearing of yourselves ~ defense

clearing ~ acquitting

cleave ~ cling

cleave ~ split, divide

cleaved ~ clung

cleaveth ~ cleaves: clings

cleaveth ~ cleaves: splits

cleft ~ split

clemency ~ mercy, mildness

clift ~ hole, crevice

clifts ~ older form of clefts: spaces made by cleaving (splitting); *Heb* chasms, ravines, steep slopes; clefts

climbeth ~ climbs ~ 1

cloke of covetousness ~ disguise or pretense of greed

cloke ~ cloak: veil or cover

close ~ shut-up: quiet

closest ~ close ~ 1

closet ~ small private room for reading, meditation, etc.

clothest ~ clothe ~ 1

clouted ~ patched

cloven ~ split, divided

clovenfooted ~ with a split or divided foot or hoof

coast ~ border, region, country

coasts ~ borders, regions, countries

cock crew ~ rooster crowed

cock ~ rooster

cockatrice ~ a fabulous serpent supposedly hatched from a cock's (rooster's) egg and having power to kill by a look; *Heb* poisonous snake; viper or adder (from OFr cocatris--crocodile)

cockle ~ any of various weeds that grow in grain fields: darnel, tares, weeds; *Heb* stinkweed

coffer ~ chest, box, trunk, or coffin

cogitations ~ thoughts, reflections, considerations, or meditations

college ~ building used for worship or education; educational or religious building

collops ~ folds of fatty flesh on the body

colour ~ color ~ 14

coloured ~ colored ~ 1

colours ~ colors ~ 12

come by ~ control, secure
comeliness ~ *Heb* ornament, splendor, majesty; honor, glory; *Gk* charm or excellence of figure, external beauty, decorum, modesty, seemliness
comely ~ beautiful, pretty, fair, pleasing; appropriate, fitting, becoming; *Arc* seemly, decorous, proper
comest ~ come ~ 29
cometh ~ comes ~ 282
comfortedst ~ comforted ~ 1
comforteth ~ comforts ~ 5
commandedst ~ commanded ~ 4
commandest ~ command ~ 3
commandeth ~ commands ~ 13
commend ~ entrust; recommend; *Gk* demonstrate, display, exhibit
commended of ~ praised by
commended ~ entrusted
commendeth ~commends: recommends; praises; demonstrates, displays
commending ~ recommending
commit sacrilege ~ rob temples i.e. plunder pagan shrines
committest ~ commit ~ 1
committeth ~ commits ~ 19
commodious ~ suitable, convenient
commotions ~ *Arc* civil uprisings
commune ~ converse, i.e. communicate, talk, speak
communed ~ conversed; i.e. communicated, talked, spoke
communicate ~ impart, give, share, confer; convey knowledge, information, or something tangible; *Gk* fellowship, become a partaker together
communicated ~ imparted, gave, shared, conferred; conveyed knowledge, information, or something tangible; *Gk* fellowshiped, became a partaker together
communication ~ sharing; *Gk* fellowship
communications ~ *Gk* words: conversations; *Gk* companionships, communion (homilia)
companied ~ *Arc* associated
company ~ *Arc* associate
compass thee round ~ *Arc* surround, circle; encompass thee
compass ~ *Arc* circled, went around; took a detour
compass ~ *Arc* circle; go around; encompass; surround
compass ~ *Arc* circumference, enclosed area or space, width (*Heb* edge, rim)
compassed ~ *Arc* encircled, enclosed; encompassed; surrounded; went/gone around
compassed about ~ *Arc* encircled, enclosed; surrounded; went around
compassest ~ compass: *Arc* encircle, enclose; surround; go around
compasseth ~ compasses: *Arc* encircles, encloses; surrounds; goes around
compassing ~ *Arc* encircling, enclosing; surrounding
compellest ~ force
compellest ~ compel ~ 1
compoundeth ~ compounds ~ 1
comprehended ~ understood, mentally grasped; included, comprised; *Gk* summarized
concealeth ~ conceals ~ 2
conceit ~ opinion
conceits ~ opinions
concerneth ~ concerns ~ 2

concision ~ cutting off or mutilation; division or schism

concluded ~ _Gk_ enclosed

concord ~ agreement, harmony; (from root "same heart/ mind"); _Gk_ concord, agreement: sumphonAsis

concourse ~ assembly of people, crowd, throng, gathering; a large open area or hall where a crowd gathers; (from root meaning "running together")

concubine ~ secondary wife--inferior socially and legally

concubines ~ secondary wives-- inferior socially and legally

concupiscence ~ strong desire or appetite, esp. sexual desire-- lust; lasciviousness, eroticism, lechery

condemned ~ punished, fined

condemnest ~ condemn ~ 1

condemneth ~ condemns: slights, scorns, despises, or treats with contempt

condescend to ~ descend voluntarily to the level of

conduct him forth ~ _Obs_ escort him

conducted ~ lead, guided

conduit ~ pipe or channel for carrying fluid

coney ~ small, rabbit-like nocturnal animal that lives in rock holes; perhaps a hyrax

· **confection** ~ something mixed together; a concoction; _Heb_ a spice mixture

confectionaries ~ ones who mix things together; concoction makers; _Heb_ ointment-makers, perfumers, spice-mixers

confederacy ~ union, alliance; people or group united for some common purpose

confederate ~ united, allied

confesseth ~ confesses ~ 3

confirmeth ~ confirms ~ 3

confound ~ confuse, perplex; _Arc_ destroy

confounded ~ confused, perplexed; ashamed, disgraced; bewildered

congealed ~ thickened, coagulated, jelled

conies ~ small, rabbit-like nocturnal animals that live in rock holes; perhaps hyraxes

consecrated ~ set apart as holy

consentedst ~ consented ~ 1

considerest ~ consider ~ 2

considereth ~ considers ~ 9

consist ~ _Arc_ hold together

consisteth ~ consists ~ 1

consolation ~ comfort

consorted ~ associated, kept company

constantly ~ continually

constrain ~ compel, force, oblige, or strongly encourage

constrained ~ compelled, forced, obliged, or strongly encouraged

constraineth ~ constrains: compels, forces, obliges, or strongly encourages

constraint ~ compulsion, force, obligation

consulteth ~ consults ~ 1

consumeth ~ consumes ~ 4

consumption ~ wasting away of the body; a disease that causes this, esp tuberculosis of the lungs; destruction

contain ~ exercise self-control

containeth ~ contains ~ 1

contemn ~ slight, scorn disdain, despise, or treat with contempt
contemned ~ scorned, disdained, despised, treated with contempt
contemneth ~ contemns ~ 1
contemptible ~ utterly despised or scorned
contemptuously ~ scornfully
contend ~ dispute, debate, fight
contended ~ disputed, argued, fought
contendest ~ contend: dispute
contendeth ~ contends ~ 3
contention ~ discord, conflict, dispute, strife; controversy, quarrel
contention ~ struggle
contention ~
contentions ~ conflicts, disputes, quarrels
contentious ~ always ready to argue; quarrelsome
continueth ~ continues ~ 5
contradiction ~ opposition
contrariwise ~ on the other hand, on the contrary
contrary ~ opposed, antagonistic; unfavorable; opposite
convenient ~ appropriate, suitable fitting
conversant among ~ familiar or acquainted with
conversant ~ acquainted   .
conversation ~ behavior, conduct, manner of life; *Gk* citizenship, commonwealth
converted ~ changed, transformed
converteth ~ converts ~ 1
conveyed ~ transported, taken
convince ~ prove guilty, vanquish, refute

convinced ~ proved guilty, vanquished, refuted
convinceth ~ convicts, proves guilty
convinceth ~ convinces ~ 1
convocation ~ group called together; assembly, gathering
coping ~ top layer of masonry wall
coppersmith ~ artisan who makes or repairs copper objects, esp by shaping the metal while it is hot and soft   .
cormorant ~ large voracious sea bird
corn ~ grain (various types); kernel
cornet ~ small horn
cornets ~ small horns
cornfloor ~ grain floor; *Heb* threshing floor, barn floor
correcteth ~ corrects ~ 2
corrupt ~ debase; deceitfully peddle
corrupt ~ *Gk* corrupted & unfit for use; rotten
corrupteth ~ corrupts ~ 1
corruptible ~ perishable
costliness ~ abundance of costly things
cotes ~ small shelters or sheds for fowl, sheep, doves, etc
couch ~ crouch or lie down
couch ~ (portable) bed or couch: i.e. cot
couched ~ crouched or lay down
coucheth ~ couches ~ 1
couchingplace ~ resting place
could skill of ~ *Obs* have skill with
couldest ~ could ~ 5
coulter ~ alt of colter: vertical iron blade in front of plow
coulters ~ alt spell of colters: iron blades in front of a plow that make a vertical cut in the soil

council ~ advisers (of a Roman official); *Gk* Great Council or Sanhedrin

councils ~ assemblies of judges

counsel ~ purpose, will; *Arc* intention, resolution, purpose

counsel ~ advise

counsellor ~ counselor: advisor; *Gk* member of the Sanhedrin; senator

count ~ consider, think, account

counted ~ considered

countenance ~ i.e. facial expression: attitude; i.e. favor

countervail ~ counteract, counterbalance; compensate for; equal in value; match

counteth ~ counts ~ 3

coupled ~ joined

coupleth ~ couples: joins

course ~ way, path; i.e. turn; opportunity to run, flow, or move; i.e. organizational unit, division

courses ~ i.e. organizational divisions; shifts

covenant ~ treaty; binding, solemn agreement

covenanted ~ solemnly agreed

coveredst ~ covered ~ 2

coverest ~ cover ~ 2

covereth ~ covers ~ 27

covert ~ covered or protected place; shelter or hiding place

covet ~ ardently want; long for with envy; earnestly desire

coveted after ~ greedily longed for

coveted ~ enviously longed for

coveteth ~ covets ~ 2

covetous ~ greedy (one[s])

covetous ~ greedy, grasping

covetousness ~ insatiable (unsatisfied) desire for more; greed

cracknels ~ light, crisp biscuits

craft ~ trade

craft ~ guile; slyness; deception, trickery

craveth ~ craves ~ 1

createth ~ creates ~ 1

creature ~ created (thing); creation

creditor ~ one to whom a debt is owed

creepeth ~ creeps ~ 14

crew ~ crowed

crib ~ rack, trough, or box for fodder; manger

criest ~ cry ~ 5

crieth ~ cries ~ 17

crime laid against him ~ *Gk* accusation

crisping pins ~ curling pins for the hair

crookbackt ~ crook backed; hunch-backed; hump-backed

crop ~ sacklike enlargement of a bird's gullet where food

croucheth ~ crouches ~ 1

crownedst ~ crowned ~ 1

crownest ~ crown ~ 1

crowneth ~ crowns ~ 1

cruse ~ small vessel for liquids

cry ~ outcry, shout

cubit ~ c. 18 to 22 inches

cubits ~ each cubit= c. 18 to 22 inches

cuckow ~ *Heb* meaning unknown; possibly an extinct bird; perhaps a seagull

cumbered ~ encumbered, overwhelmed, troubled, burdened

cumbereth ~ cumbers: encumbers, burdens, hinders, obstructs

cumbrance ~ troublesome burden, encumbrance, hindrance

cummin ~ plant with bitter, warm-tasting seeds

cunning ~ Adj--skillful, clever; sly, crafty;

cunning ~ Noun--skill; craftiness, slyness

cunningly ~ cleverly

curious ~ carefully, intricately, or skillfully made; highly detailed or elaborate in workmanship

cursedst ~ cursed ~ 2

cursest ~ curse ~ 1

curseth ~ curses ~ 10

custom ~ tribute, tax, toll

cuttest ~ cut ~ 1

cutteth ~ cuts ~ 6

dainties ~ choice foods, delicacies

dainty ~ delicious, choice; delicately pretty or lovely

dale ~ valley

dam ~ mother of an animal; mother (variant of dame--lady)

damnation ~ condemnation; doom; consignment to eternal punishment (from Fr damn--condemn); *Gk* judgment

damned ~ condemned; doomed; consigned to eternal punishment (from Fr damn--condemn)

damsel ~ girl, maiden

damsels ~ girls, maidens

dandled ~ danced up and down

darkeneth ~ darkens ~ 1

darling ~ beloved; favorite; one and only (from O.E. deorling: "dearling" diminutive of dear)

dart ~ pointed missile: dart, arrow, javelin

darts ~ sharp-pointed weapons: arrows, spears

dash ~ smash

dasheth ~ dashes ~ 2

daub ~ cover, coat, or plaster with any substance

daubed ~ covered, coated, or plastered with any substance

daubing ~ coating, plaster

daysman ~ mediator, arbiter, umpire

dayspring ~ daybreak, sun-rising, early dawn

deal ~ portion, share, part, allotment

deal ~ distribute

dealest ~ deal ~ 2

dealeth ~ deals ~ 10

deals ~ portions, parts

dearth ~ drought, famine (lack or scarcity of anything, esp food)

debase ~ reduce in value, quality, dignity, rank or position

decayeth ~ decays ~ 3

decease ~ death

deceased ~ died

deceivableness ~ deceit, deception, deceitfulness

deceiveth ~ deceives ~ 6

deck ~ adorn, decorate; cover, clothe (with finery or ornaments)

decked ~ adorned, decorated; covered, clothed (with finery or ornaments)

deckedst ~ decked: adorned, decorated; covered, clothed (with finery or ornaments)

deckest ~ deck: adorn, decorate; cover, clothe (with finery or ornaments)

decketh ~ decks: adorns, decorates; covers, clothes (with finery or ornaments)

declare ~ explain, interpret

declareth ~ declares ~ 4

decline ~ deviate, diverge, turn away from, fall away from

declined ~ deviated, diverged, turned from, fallen from

declineth ~ declines: deviates, diverges, turns from, falls from

deep ~ Poetic: the sea or the ocean

defendest ~ defend ~ 1

defer ~ delay, postpone

deferred ~ postponed, delayed, put off

deferreth ~ defers: delays

defiledst ~ defiled ~ 1

defileth ~ defiles ~ 9

defraud ~ take away, deprive, or withhold property, rights, etc. by fraud; cheat, rob

defrauded ~ taken away, deprived, or withheld property or rights by fraud

degree ~ step, status, or standing

delayeth ~ delays ~ 2

delectable ~ delightful, pleasing, delicious

deliciously ~ luxuriously, sensually, wantonly

delightest ~ delight ~ 1

delighteth ~ delights ~ 14

delightsome ~ delightful, pleasurable, enjoyable

deliveredst ~ delivered ~ 3

deliverest ~ deliver ~ 2

delivereth ~ delivers ~ 13

delusion ~ false belief

demanded of ~ i.e. interrogated in a demanding way by

denieth ~ denies ~ 4

denounce ~ *Obs* announce, esp in a menacing way

departed asunder ~ went apart; *Gk* separated

departed ~ *Obs* divided in two

departeth ~ departs ~ 8

deputed ~ appointed, assigned, authorized

deride ~ ridicule, scorn, mock, make fun of

derided ~ ridiculed, scorned, mocked, made fun of

derision ~ ridicule, scorn, contempt; object of ridicule, scorn, contempt

descend ~ come or go down

descended ~ went or came down

descendeth ~ descends ~ 1

descending ~ going or coming down

descent ~ downward slope

describe ~ divide, delineate, trace the form or outline of

described ~ divided, delineated, outlined, traced

describeth ~ describes ~ 2

description ~ division, delineation, outline

descry ~ observe; spy out, put under surveillance; search out

desert ~ deserted, uninhabited

deserts ~ deserted or uninhabited (places)

deserveth ~ deserves ~ 1

desired to tarry ~ encouraged to stay

desired ~ summoned or called for; asked; i.e. asked a

desiredst ~ desired ~ 2

desirest ~ desire ~ 2

desireth ~ desires ~ 17

desirous of vain glory ~ eager for empty praise

desolate ~ uninhabited, deserted; barren, lifeless, alone

desolation ~ devastation, ruin

despise dominion ~ view authority with contempt

despise ~ scorn, hate, detest; look down upon with contempt or scorn

despised ~ hated, scorned, detested; looked down on with contempt; disregarded, rejected

despisers of ~ haters that look down upon

despisest thou ~ *Gk* do you think little or nothing of

despisest ~ despise ~ 1

despiseth ~ despises: looks down on with contempt & scorn; disregards; *Gk* rejects, refuses

despite ~ *Arc* contempt, scorn, spitefulness

despiteful ~ *Arc* spiteful, malicious

despitefully ~ *Arc* spitefully, maliciously

destitute ~ completely lacking, devoid, empty, poverty-stricken; *Obs* abandoned, forsaken

destroyest ~ destroy ~ 4

destroyeth ~ destroys ~ 8

determinate ~ settled, decided; conclusive

devices ~ plans: evil schemes or tricks

devil ~ demon, evil spirt; *Gk* diabolis slanderer, devil: metaphorical (one devil, many demons)

devilish ~ demon-like

devils ~ demons, evil spirits; (*Heb* hairy ones; satyrs)

deviseth ~ devises ~ 8

devotions ~ *Gk* objects of worship, i.e. idols, altars, temples

devourest ~ devour ~ 1

devoureth ~ devours ~ 10

diadem ~ royal crown; crown-like ornamental headband

dial ~ i.e. sun-dial

did very abominably ~ acted in a very vile, loathsome, detestable, disgusting, or hateful manner

diddest ~ did ~ 1

didst ~ did ~ 122

diest ~ die ~ 1

dieth ~ dies ~ 30

differeth ~ differs ~ 2

diggedst ~ digged, ~ dug ~ 1

diggeth ~ digs ~ 3

dignities ~ *Arc* dignitaries: persons holding a high, dignified position

dined ~ eaten dinner

dippeth ~ dips ~ 2

directeth ~ directs ~ 3

dirt ~ excrement

disallow ~ refuses to allows; rejects as untrue, invalid

disallowed ~ disapproved; rejected, repudiated

disannul ~ completely cancel, annul, nullify

disannuleth ~ disannuls: completely cancels, annuls, nullifies

disannulled ~ completely canceled, annulled, nullified

disannulling ~ complete canceling, annulling, nullifying

disappointeth ~ disappoints ~ 1

discerned ~ examined, discerned; recognized

discerneth ~ discerns ~ 1

discharged ~ unloaded

discomfited ~ *Arc* defeated, routed, put to flight; destroyed

discomfiture ~ *Arc* defeat, rout

discord ~ lack of harmony, dissension, conflict

discover ~ *Arc* reveal, expose, uncover

discovered ~ *Arc* uncovered, displayed, exposed, revealed; *Arc* sighted

discovereth ~ discovers: *Arc* uncovers, displays, exposes, reveals

disguiseth ~ disguises ~ 1

dishonour ~ dishonor ~ 11

dishonourest ~ dishonor ~ 1

dishonoureth ~ dishonors ~ 3

dismayed ~ afraid, troubled; alarmed

disorderly ~ in a lawless, unruly, disorderly way

dispensation ~ stewardship, economy, administration, management

dispersed abroad ~ distributed widely

dispersed ~ scattered

disposed ~ inclined, willing

disposition ~ arrangement, means

disputation ~ discussion; debate; dispute, argument, quarrel

disputations ~ discussions; debates; disputes, arguments

disputed ~ debated, argued

disputer ~ debater

disputing ~ *Gk* discussion, disputation

disputings ~ arguments

disquiet ~ disturb, distress, trouble; make anxious, uneasy, restless

disquieted ~ distressed, troubled; made anxious, restless

disquietness ~ distress; anxiety, restlessness

dissembled ~ disguised or concealed real nature, motives, or feelings behind a false appearance; behaved hypocritically

dissemblers ~ hypocrites; pretenders

dissembleth ~ dissembles: acts hypocritically; disguises or conceals real nature, motives, feelings behind a false appearance

dissension ~ strife, violent wrangling; violent quarreling; i.e. riot

dissimulation ~ hypocrisy, duplicity, deception

dissolvest ~ dissolve ~ 1

dissolving ~ ending

distaff ~ staff on which fibers, as flax, wool or tow, are wound before being spun into thread

distil ~ fall in drops, trickle, drip

distress ~ necessity or distress

distributeth ~ distributes ~ 1

divers ~ different, various, several (ones) ·

diverse ~ different

diversities ~ differences

divideth ~ divides ~ 10

divination ~ prediction by magic; the act or practice of trying to foretell the future or explore the unknown by occult means

divine ~ foretell the future by occult means; prophesy (through occult means)

divine divinations ~ prophesy by occult means

diviners ~ foretellers of the future or the unknown by occult means

divineth ~ practices divination, foretells the future

divineth ~ divines ~ 1

divining ~ foretelling future by occult means

divorcement ~ divorce

do iniquity ~ *Gk* practice lawlessness

do err ~ do wrong, deviate from the right

do ~ i.e. want

doctors ~ teachers or learned men

doest ~ do ~ 45

doeth ~ does ~ 96

doleful ~ sorrowful, mournful, gloomy

dominion ~ sovereign authority, power, or rule; lordship

dominions ~ sovereign lordships

done ~ i.e. finished

dost ~ do ~ 56

dote ~ say, think, or do foolishly; become foolish

doted ~ had a foolish or excessive affection or lust

doth ~ does ~ 207

doting ~ having a foolish or excessive fondness

doubletongued ~ deceitful or insincere in speech

doubted of ~ was uncertain about

doubteth ~ doubts ~ 1

doubtless ~ without a doubt; at least, truly, indeed

downsitting ~ sitting down

dowry ~ money paid to wife as divorce security; gift, endowment; *Arc* gift from a man to his bride

drag ~ dragnet

dragon ~ *Obs* Bible a word used to translate one Hebrew word meaning dragon or dinosaur; sea or river monster; or serpent or venomous snake

dragons ~ *Obs* Bible a word used to translate one Hebrew word (15x) meaning dragons or dinosaurs; sea or river monsters; or serpents or venomous snakes A second Hebrew word is rendered dragon only in Mal 3:1. It's meaning is uncertain: dragons, jackals, sea monsters (??)

drams ~ lit. handful, then a weight or coin, and finally a measure; weight today=1/16 oz (about 5/16 oz in Bible times)

draught ~ Brit spell for draft: a drawing in of a fish net; the amount of fish caught in one draw

draught ~ privy, toilet, sewer

drave ~ drove: drove (*Arc* spelling)

draw ~ drag

drawers ~ haulers

draweth ~ draws ~ 12

dreameth ~ dreams ~ 2

dress ~ prepare: clean and eviscerate (an animal)

dressed ~ prepared: cleaned and eviscerated (for eating); cultivated

dresser ~ caretaker

dresseth ~ dresses: prepares (for use); trims

drew ~ dragged

drewest ~ drew ~ 1

driedst ~ dried ~ 1

drieth ~ dries ~ 3

drinketh ~ drinks ~ 17

driveth ~ drives ~ 4

dromedaries ~ one-humped Arabian camels, esp ones trained for fast riding

dromedary ~ one-humped Arabian camel, esp one trained for fast riding

droppeth ~ drops ~ 1

drove ~ animals moving as a group: flock, herd

dryshod ~ with dry shoes

due season ~ proper time; *Gk* our own time

due ~ proper; *Gk* his own

due benevolence ~ required "kindness" i.e. conjugal duty

dues ~ debts

duke ~ chief, leader, noble

dukes ~ chiefs, leaders, noblemen

dulcimer ~ *Heb* meaning uncertain: stringed instrument or any instrument making a pleasant sound [?]

dumb ~ voiceless, mute

dung ~ refuse, waste matter; manure, excrement; or anything morally filthy

dung ~ fertilize with dung, manure, refuse

dunghill ~ heap or pile of refuse, waste matter, manure, excrement

dunghills ~ heaps or piles of refuse, waste matter, manure, excrement

dureth ~ *Arc* form of endures: lasts, continues, persists

dureth ~ dures>endures ~ 1

durst ~ dares to; dared

durst ~ dare ~ 9

dwell ~ live

dwellest ~ live

dwellest ~ dwell ~ 19

dwelleth ~ dwells: lives

dwelt ~ lived

ear ~ plow [*Arc*]

ear ~ grain or seed bearing spike of cereal plant, esp corn

eared ~ tilled, plowed

earing ~ plowing or plowing time [*Arc*]

early ~ in the near future; *Heb* early, earnestly, diligently

earnest ~ down payment: money paid in advance as part payment to bind a contract or bargain; promise or assurance: a token of something to come

earneth ~ earns ~ 2

earthen vessels ~ clay containers

Easter ~ Ishtar--ancient pagan festival: from ME ester (spring) and Eastre (dawn goddess); Easter was originally the name of a pagan spring festival that occurred at about the same time as the Passover. *Gk* passover

easy to be intreated ~ *Gk* compliant

eatest ~ eat ~ 3

eateth ~ eats ~ 56

edification ~ building up

edified ~ built up

edifieth ~ edifies: builds up

edify not ~ don't build up

edify ~ build up (morally or spiritually)

edifying ~ building up

effect ~ accomplish

effect ~ result (*Heb* service, labor, work)

effect ~ "maketh . . . Of none effect"=frustrates, restrains

effect ~ "spake . . . To that [effect]"= spoke . . .about this

effect ~ accomplishment, result; i.e. fulfillment

effect ~ force, influence, or power

effect ~ "made . . . Of none effect" = nullified, canceled

effect ~ "making . . . Of none effect"= nullifying

effectual ~ effective; fully adequate

effectually ~ effectively; fully adequately

effeminate ~*Gk* lit: soft, soft to the touch; fig (in a bad sense): effeminate--of a catamite (a boy sexually used by an adult pedophile); of a boy kept for homosexual relations with a man; of a male who submits his body to unnatural lewdness; of a male prostitute

elders ~ *Gk* presbuterion: body of elders, senate

elect ~ chosen (ones)

elect's ~ chosen one's

elected ~ chosen

election ~ choice, choosing, selection

elements ~ elementary principles, basics

Elias ~ Elijah ~ 30

else ~ otherwise

emboldened ~ made bold or bolder; given courage, encouraged

emboldeneth ~ emboldens: makes bold; gives courage, encourages, incites

emerods ~ *Arc* related to hemorrhoids=blood+flow; *Heb* tumors, hemorrhoids; (ulcers??)

eminent ~ high, lofty; towering, prominent

emulation ~ desire or ambition to equal or surpass; *Obs* ambitious rivalry, envious dislike

encampeth ~ encamps ~ 2

enchantment ~ magic spells, or charms

endamage ~ inflict damage upon; injure; discredit

endeavour ~ endeavor ~ 1

endeavoured ~ endeavored: tried

endeavouring ~ endeavoring: striving, trying

endeavours ~ endeavors ~ 1

endeth ~ ends ~ 1

endow ~ pay the required dowry price for

endued ~ supplied, provided, endowed; Rare: clothed

endureth ~ endures ~ 59

engines ~ machines, instruments; apparatuses

engrafted ~ implanted; firmly established or planted

engraven ~ carved, engraved

enjoin ~ urge or impose with authority and emphasis: command, order

enjoined ~ urged or imposed with authority and emphasis: commanded, ordered

enlarged ~ magnified

enlargement ~ *Arc* release from confinement or bondage (*Heb* relief)

enlargeth ~ enlarges ~ 3

enmity ~ hostility, strong hatred

enquirest ~ enquire, ~ inquire ~ 1

enrichest ~ enrich ~ 1

ensample ~ *Arc* of example: sample, pattern, model

ensamples ~ *Arc* of examples: samples, patterns, models

ensign ~ flag, banner, or standard, esp a military one raised high as a rallying point for troops

ensigns ~ flags, banners, or standards, esp a military ones raised high as a rallying point for troops

ensue ~ *Arc* pursue, follow, strive for

entangleth ~ entangles ~ 1

entereth ~ enters ~ 20

enterprise ~ an undertaking or project, esp a difficult, bold, dan-gerous, or important one

enticeth ~ entices ~ 1

enticing ~ pleasing, alluring

entreat ~ *Arc* treat, behave toward

entreated ~ *Arc* treated; behaved toward

entreateth ~ entreats ~ 1

enviest ~ envy ~ 1

envieth ~ envies ~ 1

environ ~ surround, encircle, encompass

ephah ~ ancient Hebrew unit of dry measure estimated at from 1/3 bu to 1+ bu (8 gal or 36L)

ephod ~ richly embroidered outer vestment worn by Jewish priests; shoulder cape; mantle

epistle ~ letter, esp a long, formal, instructive one

epistles ~ letters, esp long, formal, instructive ones

equality ~ fairness, equity, equality

equity ~ fairness, impartiality, justice

ere ~ *Arc* before, until

err ~ do wrong, swerve, deviate, or wander from what is right; fall into error; go astray; commit an error

errand ~ purpose or object for being sent: mission, message

erred ~ swerved, gone astray; done wrong

erreth ~ errs ~ 2

Esaias ~ Isaiah

escapeth ~ escapes ~ 6

eschew ~ avoid; shun; abstain from; keep away from

eschewed ~ avoided; shunned; abstained from; kept from

escheweth ~ eschews: avoids; shuns; abstains from; keeps away from

espied ~ spied, caught sight of; watched; saw

espousals ~ betrothals, engagements; weddings

espoused ~ betrothed, engaged, promised in marriage; taken as a spouse, especially as a wife; married

espy ~ spy, catch sight of; see

establisheth ~ establishes ~ 3

estate ~ state, status, condition; place, office; property, possessions

estates ~ i.e. nobles

esteem other ~ consider or value the other

esteem ~ *Obs* value

esteemed ~ valued, respected

esteemeth ~ esteems ~ 4

esteeming ~ considering, valuing

estranged ~ made foreign, removed, alienated; separated; kept away

eunuch ~ (castrated or emasculated) male employed as a chamberlain or high officer by an Oriental potentate

even ~ *Arc* evening

eveningtide ~ *Arc* evening

eventide ~ *Arc* evening

ever a lover ~ always a friend

ever ~ forever; always

ever ~ ere: before

evermore ~ emphatic synonym of ever: always, continually

evident token ~ clear sign, plain proof

evident ~ clear, plain

evidently ~ clearly, plainly

evil eye ~ green-eyed jealousy or bewitching stare

evil affected ~ negatively influenced

evil ~ i.e. diseased

evilfavoredness ~ {*Arc*} deformity, ugliness; (*Heb* injury)

ewe ~ female sheep

ewes ~ female sheep

exact usury ~ require at (excessively high) interest

exact ~ force payment, practice extortion; require, demand

exacted ~ required or forced payment of

exacteth ~ exacts ~ 1

exactions ~ forced payments; extortions

exactors ~ {*Arc*} taskmasters; (oppressors; extortioners)

exaltest ~ exalt ~ 1

exalteth ~ exalts ~ 9

examination had ~ *Gk* completing a preliminary investigation

examined of ~ questioned or interrogated about

examined ~ interrogated, questioned

exceedest ~ exceed ~ 1

exceedeth ~ exceeds ~ 1

exceeding ~ *Arc* of exceedingly: extremely, surpassing, very; *Arc* very great

exceedingly ~ extremely, beyond measure, to a great degree; greatly, loudly

exceedingly the **more** ~ extremely more

excellency ~ excellence; superiority; *Gk* elevation, pre-eminence, superiority

excellent ~ *Gk* majestic

excellest ~ excel ~ 1

excelleth ~ excels ~ 3

except ~ *Arc* unless, i.e. if; but;

exchangers ~ *Obs* money chargers, exchange brokers, bankers (*Gk* those who exchange money for a fee and pay interest on deposits)

execration ~ curse

execute ~ carry out, perform

executed ~ carried out, performed

executed ~ performed, carried out

executedst ~ executed ~ 1

executest ~ execute ~ 1

executeth ~ executes ~ 6

executing ~ performing, carrying out, doing

exercised thereby ~ trained by it

exerciseth ~ exercises ~ 1

exhort ~ urge, strongly encourage; warn

exhortation ~ encouragement, warning

exhorted ~ encouraged, warned

exhorteth ~ exhorts ~ 1

exhorting ~ urgently instructing, or warning

expecting ~ expectantly waiting

expedient ~ advantageous, profitable; needful; useful or suited for the purpose or situation

expelled ~ threw or forced (out)

experiment ~ trial, test

expired ~ ended

expounded ~ explained, interpreted

extendeth ~ extends ~ 1

extol ~ praise highly

extolled ~ praised

extortioner ~ one using threats or force to get money

extortioners ~ ones using threats or force to get money

eyeservice ~ service done only while the master sees; work done only in master's sight

fadeth ~ fades ~ 7

faileth ~ fails: is lacking or deficient

fain ~ *Arc* willingly, gladly, with eagerness

faint not ~ *Arc* don't lose courage, strength, or hope

faint ~ *Arc* lose strength, courage or hope

faintest ~ faint ~ 1
fainteth ~ faints ~ 4
fair ~ lovely, attractive, beautiful, good-looking
fairs ~ markets, bazaars: scheduled gatherings of people for bartering, trading, or selling goods
fall not out ~ don't quarrel, argue, or fight
fallen asleep ~ i.e. dead
fallest ~ fall ~ 1
falleth out ~ occurs, arises
falleth ~ falls: i.e. belongs
fallow deer ~ a small Eurasian deer (Dama dama) having a yellowish-red coat spotted with white in summer and broad, flattened antlers in the male
fallowdeer ~ fallow deer: a small Eurasian deer (Dama dama) having a yellowish-red coat spotted with white in summer and broad, flattened antlers in the male
fame abroad ~ rumor or report far & wide
fame ~ *Arc* public report, rumor
familiar spirits ~ demons supposed to be in association with or under the power of a man
familiar spirit ~ demon supposed to be in association with or under the power of a man
fan ~ winnow grain with a fork-like instrument; scatter with a fork-like winnowing instrument
fan ~ fork-like instrument for winnowing
fanners ~ scatterers, winnowers
far spent ~ i.e. almost over

fare ye well ~ *Gk* prosper: farewell (letters)
fare ~ do
fared sumptuously ~ feasted magnificently
farthing ~ lit. "little fourth"; an old British coin worth a fourth of a penny; thing of little value; small piece of anything
farthings ~ lit. "little fourths"; old British coins worth a fourth of a penny
fashion ~ manner: bearing, actions, way of life
fashioneth ~ fashions ~ 3
fashioning ~ patterning, conforming
fast ~ specifically: the Day of Atonement
fast ~ *Obs* close, near
fast ~ abstain from food (entirely or partially) as a religious observance or a sign of grief
fast ~ firm
fast ~ firmly, fixedly; firmly fastened; firmly to; rapidly
fasted ~ abstained from food
fastest ~ fast ~ 1
fasting ~ abstaining from food; with no food
fastings ~ food-deprivations, starvations
fat ~ i.e. choicest, best part; abundance (of produce); i.e. thick, healthy, stout, robust; fig. the best, good
fat ones ~ *Heb* fatlings
fat ~ i.e. prosperous; i.e. rich, plentiful, abundant; i.e. fruitful, fertile; *Heb* vigorous, stalwart ones
fat ~ i.e. richly prepared food

fatfleshed ~ fat + fleshed: fat, plump; fatter

fathers ~ forefathers

fathoms ~ one fathom is c. 6 feet

fatling ~ calf, lamb, kid, or young pig fattened for slaughter

fatlings ~ calves, lambs, kids, or young pigs fattened for slaughter

fatness ~ i.e. plenty, prosperity; i.e. choice or best portions

fats ~ *Arc* vessels of large size for liquids: tubs; dyers or brewers vats; wine casks (*Heb* wine vats, wine-presses)

fattest ~ i.e. best, choicest

fault ~ *Gk* falling beside or near; lapse or deviation from truth or righteousness; misdeed; sin

favour ~ favor ~ 70

favourable ~ favorable ~ 4

favoured ~ favored ~ 14

favourest ~ favour, ~ favor ~ 1

favoureth ~ favours, ~ favors ~ 1

fearest ~ fear ~ 3

feareth ~ fears ~ 20

feeble ~ weak

feebleminded ~ *Arc* faint-hearted

feedest ~ feed ~ 2

feedeth ~ feeds ~ 8

feign ~ pretend; disguise or conceal; act or allege falsely

feigned ~ pretended; deceitful, counterfeit; hypocritical

feignedly ~ deceptively, falsely, hypocritically

feignest ~ *Arc* feign: pretend; fabricate, make-up

fell on sleep ~ fell asleep: i.e. died

fell asleep ~ i.e. died

fell a lusting ~ i.e. began to lust

fell ~ i.e. chop down

felled ~ i.e. chopped down

feller ~ lumberjack, tree-chopper

fellest ~ fell ~ 1

felling ~ chopping down

felloes ~ the curved pieces of wood which, joined together, form the circular rim of a spoked wheel; exterior rims of spoked wheels (alt fellies)

fellows ~ associates, companions, partners

fenced ~ defenced, i.e. walled

fens ~ swamps, marshes, bogs; wetlands

fervent mind ~ zeal

fervent ~ burning: zealous, ardent; intensely devoted or earnest

fervently ~ intensely, earnestly

fetch a compass ~ *Arc* circle or go around; take a circular course

fetch ~ bring; get; retrieve

fetched a compass of ~ *Arc* circled or went around; made a detour for

fetched ~ brought, retrieved, got(ten)

fetcheth ~ fetches: brings i.e. makes

fetcht ~ fetched: brought, retrieved, got

fetters ~ shackles, metal bands, or chains for the feet (or hands)

fidelity ~ faithfulness

fighteth ~ fights ~ 3

figure ~ figure of speech, type, metaphor, emblem; *Gk* parable

figures ~ *Gk* anti-types

filledst ~ filled ~ 2

fillest ~ fill ~ 1

fillet ~ flat square molding separating other moldings; narrow band between two grooves in a column

filleted ~ ornamented with encircling bands

filleth ~ fills ~ 6

fillets ~ flat square moldings separating other moldings; narrow bands between two grooves or flutings in a column

filthy lucre ~ illicit, dishonorable, or unlawful gain or advantage

findest ~ find ~ 2

findeth ~ finds ~ 27

fine ~ shortened form of refine: refine, purify

finer ~ refiner, smelter, silver (or gold) smith

fining ~ refining (fining pot=crucible)

firebrands ~ pieces of burning wood

firkins ~ lit "fourths": each firkin=1/4 barrel--a little less than 9 English gallons

firmament ~ sky, viewed poetically as a solid arch or vault; the vault or expanse of the heavens

firstbegotten ~ first-born; first-fathered

firstling ~ firstborn, first of a kind

firstlings ~ firstborn ones, first ones of a kind

fitches ~ vetches: vicia sativa (or nigella sativa) plants or just the small, black acrid seeds used as a seasoning; *Heb* black cumin

fitly ~ properly, suitably

fitted to ~ suited, adapted, prepared for

fitteth ~ fits ~ 1

fixed ~ un-movable, firmly fixed; established, steadfast; steady

flag ~ marshland plant: reed, rush, cattail, iris

flagon ~ *Heb* raisin-cake, used in sacrificial feasts

flagons ~ earthen or skin containers; jugs, jars; skin-bags

flagons ~ "flagons of wine"=raisin-cakes of grapes (used in sacrificial feasts) cf Heb

flags ~ marshland plants: reeds, rushes, cattails, irises

flanks ~ fleshy sides of an animal between the last rib and the hips: sides

flattereth ~ flatters ~ 6

flay ~ strip off the skin or hide of, as by whipping; skin

flayed ~ stripped off skin or hide of, as by whipping; skinned

fleddest ~ fled ~ 2

fleeth ~ flees ~ 8

fleshhook ~ hook for flesh; large fork

fleshhooks ~ hooks for flesh; large forks

flieth ~ flies ~ 5

flight ~ fleeing

floats ~ rafts

flourished ~ vigorously grown, thrived

flourisheth ~ flourishes ~ 2

flowers ~ *Arc* menstrual flow

floweth ~ flows ~ 12

fluttereth ~ flutters ~ 1

flux ~ any excessive or unnatural discharge of fluid body matter, esp from the bowels ("bloody flux"=*Gk* dusenteria: dysentery, bowel ailment)

foameth ~ foams ~ 2

foes ~ enemies

fold ~ times

foldeth ~ folds ~ 1

followedst ~ followed ~ 1

followeth ~ follows ~ 15

foot ~ i.e. base

footmen ~ *Arc* men who go on foot such as foot soldiers

for to ~ i.e. in order to; i.e. to; *Arc* unless

for to sojourn ~ in order to stay, dwell, or live temporarily

for that ~ instead; i.e. because; *Gk* because

for ~ because of

for all ~ i.e. although

forasmuch ~ for+as+much: since, because; inasmuch (as)

forbad ~ forbade ~ 5

forbare ~ *Arc* for forbore: ceased, stopped

forbear to help ~ refrain from helping; avoid helping

forbear ~ refrain (from), abstain (from); cease, stop, avoid; restrain; endure, tolerate

forbearance ~ toleration, patience; self-restraint

forbeareth ~ forbears: *Arc* ceases, forgoes; rejects: i.e. fails

forbearing ~ refraining from (*Gk* omitting, giving up)

forbearing ~ i.e. restraining myself, holding it in; *Gk* sustaining, holding up; enduring

forbiddeth ~ forbids ~ 1

forborn ~ ceased, hesitated

forecast ~ arrange, plan, scheme, or contrive

forefront ~ front-most part, extreme front

foreknew ~ knew before

foreknowledge ~ forethought; *Gk* foreknowledge, pre-arrangement

foremost ~ first, farthest to the front

foreordained ~ ordained or appointed beforehand

forepart ~ front part

foreseeth ~ foresees ~ 2

foreship ~ ship's bow or forward part

forgat ~ forgot ~ 8

forgavest ~ forgave ~ 2

forgettest ~ forget ~ 2

forgetteth ~ forgets ~ 4

forgiveth ~ forgives ~ 2

formeth ~ forms ~ 2

fornication ~ legally: sexual relations between unmarried persons; *Gk* any kind of illicit sexual relations

fornicator ~ *Gk* male prostitute

fornicators ~ practicers of sexual sin

forsaketh ~ forsakes ~ 6

forsomuch as ~ i.e. since, because

forsookest ~ forsook ~ 2

forswear thyself ~ renounce an oath; swear falsely, perjure thyself

forth ~ out, forward

forthwith ~ immediately, at once, without delay

forum ~ marketplace

forward ~ willing

forwardness ~ zeal, eagerness; inclination, readiness

foul ~ evil; stormy

fouledst ~ fouled ~ 1

founder ~ one who founds or casts metal or glass in a mold

foundest ~ found ~ 1

fourfold ~ four times as much; four times, i.e. with four lambs

fourscore ~ eighty (a score is 20)

foursquare ~ adj: with four equal sides; n: *Arc* square

fowl ~ flying creature(s): bird(s), flying insect(s)

fowler ~ bird-hunter

fowlers ~ bird-hunters

fowls ~ flying creatures: birds, winged insects

fragments ~ food-remnants: i.e. leftovers

frame ~ form, framework, structure

frame ~ manage; form; conform

frameth mischief ~ brings about harm, injury, damage

frameth ~ frames ~ 2

frankincense ~ aromatic gum resin burned as a fragrant incense

frankly ~ *Gk* freely, graciously

fray ~ *Arc* frighten, scare, terrify (afraid=affrayed)

fret ~ eaten away, decayed

fret ~ eat away, gnaw; irritate, vex; annoy; worry

fretted ~ worried, irritated

fretteth ~ frets: is being angry, vexed, irritated

fretting ~ eating, gnawing, or corroding

frontlets ~ things worn on the forehead: phylacteries--small leather cases holding slips inscribed with Scripture

froward ~ stubbornly willful; not easily controlled; contrary; twisted; perverted: disposed to go contrary to the reasonable or required

frowardly ~ in a stubbornly willful way

frowardness ~ stubborn willfulness; perversity; disposition to go contrary to the reasonable or required

frustrateth ~ frustrates ~

full ~ fully

fuller ~ lit. bleacher: one who fulls cloth--cleans and whitens it by stamping or beating it in a chemical solution

furbish ~ polish, brighten, brush, or clean

furbished ~ polished, brightened, brushed, or cleaned

furious ~ wildly raging, violently angry

furlongs ~ lit. long furrow: the length of a furrow in common field of 10 acres; a furlong is 1/8 of an English mile--c.200 yards

furniture ~ anything furnished or provided: furnishings, equipment, supplies (*Heb* basket saddle)

furtherance ~ advancement, progress

gaddest ~ gad: move about restlessly, roam idly

gainsay ~ speak against, contradict, oppose, hinder

gainsayers ~ speakers against, contradictors, opponents, hinderers

gainsaying ~ speaking against, contradicting, opposing, hindering; "bad-mouthing"

gall ~ something bitter or distasteful; bile; *Arc* gall-bladder

gallant ~ stately, imposing; beautiful in appearance

garlands ~ wreaths of flowers

garner ~ storehouse for grain; granary; grain-bin

garners ~ granary, place for storing grain; grain-bins

garnish ~ decorate, embellish, adorn

garnished ~ decorated, embellished, adorned

gat ~ got

gatherest ~ gather ~ 1

gathereth ~ gathers ~ 17

gave him audience ~ listened to him

gave place ~ yielded

gave suck ~ nursed
gave ear ~ listened, paid attention
gave audience ~ *Obs* gave a hearing;
 Gk listened
gavest ~ gave ~ 34
gay ~ fine (*Gk* shining, splendid,
 magnificent)
gazingstock ~ object of someone's
 stare; a spectacle; i.e. object of
 public humiliation
gender ~ *Arc* of engender: breed,
 generate, produce
gendered ~ *Arc* of engendered: bred,
 generated, produced
gendereth ~ genders: *Arc* of
 engenders--breeds, generates,
 produces, reproduces
generation of vipers ~ descendants of
 poisonous snakes
getteth ~ gets ~ 9
ghost ~ spirit
gier eagle ~ a bird of prey; maybe a
 kind of carrion vulture;
 perhaps an extinct bird; exact
 meaning unknown
gin ~ short for engine: mechanical
 device, trap, or snare
gins ~ engines: mechanical devices,
 traps, or snares
gird ~ encircle, fasten, or secure with
 a belt or band; clothe
girded ~ encircled, fastened, or
 secured with a belt or band;
 clothed
girdedst ~girded: encircled, fastened,
 or secured with a belt or band;
 clothed
girdeth ~ girds: encircles, fastens, or
 secures with a belt or band;
 clothes
girding ~ wrapping, binding
girdle ~ belt or sash worn around the
 waist

girdles ~ belts or sashes worn around
 the waist
girt ~ encircled, fastened, or secured
 with a belt or band
give in charge ~ *Gk* command
give my child suck ~ nurse my child
give place ~ make room: i.e. leave,
 withdraw; provide a place or
 opportunity
give suck ~ nurse
give thee charge ~ command you
give ear ~ listen, pay attention
give audience ~ *Gk* listen
given ~ addicted, inclined; *Gk*
 enslaved
givest ~ give ~ 12
giveth ~ gives ~ 126
giving out ~ making public; *Gk*
 saying
glad tidings ~ happy news
glass ~ mirror
glasses ~ mirrors
glean it ~ collect what has dropped
glean ~ collect the leavings from (the
 harvesting process); gather the
 produce left behind by the
 harvesters; gather what
 reapers drop
gleaned ~ gathered
gleanings ~ leavings, leftovers:
 dropped by harvesters
glede ~ lit =glide: bird of prey like a
 buzzard, kite, or hawk
glistering ~ shinning, sparkling,
 glittering (glister=*Arc* of
 glitter)
gloriest ~ glory ~ 1
glorieth ~ glories: boast(s)
glorifieth ~ glorifies ~ 1
glory of ~ rejoice in
glory ~ rejoice, boast
glorying of ~ boasting about

glorying ~ boasting

gluttonous ~ greedy for food; excessively over-eating

gnash ~ grind or chew (in anger or pain)

gnashed ~ ground or chewed (in anger or pain)

gnasheth upon him with his teeth ~ grinds his teeth at him (in anger)

gnasheth ~ gnashes: grinds or chews (in pain or fear)

gnashing ~ grinding (in pain or anger)

go to ~ *Arc* come, come on; indeed

go a whoring ~ prostitute themselves: lit. through cult prostitution to false gods or fig. by spiritual unfaithfulness to the true God

god speed ~ good success i.e. God bless you

godhead ~ Godhood, divinity, deity

gods ~ *Heb* elohim i.e. judges

goest ~ go ~ 46

goeth ~ goes ~ 135

going ~ departure (*Heb* marching, anklet)

goldsmith ~ artisan who makes or repairs gold objects, esp by shaping the metal while it is hot and soft

goldsmiths ~ artisans who make or repair gold objects, esp by shaping the metal while it is hot and soft

gone a whoring ~ prostituted themselves: lit. through cult prostitution to false gods or fig. by spiritual unfaithfulness to the true God

goodly ~ good-looking; good-quality, fine; good-sized

goodman ~ male head of household; host; husband

gopher ~ meaning and exact type unknown: cypress wood ?

governor ~ helmsman

graffed ~ grafted

grave ~ dignified, serious; sober, serious, important; somber

grave ~ engrave, carve (*Arc* of engrave)

graven ~ metal, melted and cast into a mold

graven ~ carved, sculptured; engraved

graveth ~ graves: carves

graving ~ engraving, carving (*Arc* of engraving)

gravity ~ solemnity or sedateness of manner or character; earnestness; dignity, seriousness

greater part ~ majority

greaves ~ leg-armor that covers from ankle to knee

Grecia ~ Latin for Greece

Grecians ~ Greek-speaking Jews

greeteth ~ greets ~ 1

greyhound ~ perhaps an extinct animal

grieveth ~ grieves ~ 2

grievous ~ burdensome, heavy; severe, harsh; painful; very serious; grief-producing; causing pain or grief; *Gk* cruel

grievously ~ severely, harshly, painfully

grievousness ~ harshness, severity

grisled ~ gray-colored (whole or spotted); variant of grizzled-- grizzle

groaneth ~ groans ~ 1

gropeth ~ gropes ~ 1

gross ~ thick, dense; fat, corpulent, heavy (Fr thick)

ground ~ *Obs* foundation, solid base
groweth ~ grows ~ 14
grudge ~ grumble; begrudge, be
    envious; harbor hostility; ill
    will; *Gk* sigh, groan
grudging ~ muttering, complaining;
    resentment
grudgingly ~ reluctantly
guile ~ deceit, deception, cunning,
    craftiness, trickery
gulf ~ wide, deep chasm or abyss
habergeon ~ sleeveless coat, jacket or
    poncho of protective armor
    that is shorter than a hauberk
    (*Heb* corselet: a piece of
    armor formerly worn to
    protect the trunk)
habergeons ~ sleeveless coats, jackets
    or ponchos of protective
    armor that is shorter than a
    hauberk (*Heb* corselets--
    pieces of armor formerly worn
    to protect the trunk)
habitation ~ home, dwelling place
habitations ~ dwellings; settlements
had ~ held
had in abomination with ~ viewed as
    disgusting, detestable, or
    loathsome
had in remembrance ~ remembered
had indignation ~ i.e. were angry
hadst ~ had ~ 22
haft ~ handle, hilt (that which is held)
hale ~ *Arc* draw, haul; pull with force
    or violence
haling ~ *Arc* drawing, hauling; pulling
    with force or violence
hallow ~ make holy, consecrate,
    sanctify, set apart
hallowed ~ made holy, consecrated,
    sanctified, set apart

hallowed ~ holy, consecrated,
    sanctified, set apart, purified
halt ~ *Arc* lame, crippled
halt ~ *Arc* walk with a crippled gait;
    limp; hobble
halted ~ *Arc* walked with a crippled
    gait; limped; hobbled
halteth ~ *Arc* walks with a crippled
    gait; limps; hobbles
halteth ~ halts, ~ limps ~ 2
halting ~ *Arc* walking with a crippled
    gait; limping; hobbling
handleth ~ handles ~ 3
handmaid ~ *Arc* handmaiden: female
    servant or attendant
handmaiden ~ *Arc* female servant or
    attendant
handmaidens ~ *Arc* female servants
    or attendants
handmaids ~ *Arc* handmaidens:
    female servants or attendants
handstaves ~ *Arc* staffs carried as a
    weapon: i.e. war clubs
hangeth ~ hangs ~ 2
hap ~ *Arc* chance; luck; lot
haply ~ by chance; *Arc* by chance or
    accident; perhaps
happeneth ~ happens ~ 6
hard ~ *Arc* close, near
hard by ~ *Arc* close by, near to
hardeneth ~ hardens ~ 4
hardly ~ *Rare* with difficulty or
    effort; harshly, severely
hardness ~ hardships
harlot ~ prostitute (originally a
    euphemism for whore)
harlots ~ prostitutes (originally a
    euphemism for whores)
harness ~ *Arc* armor (or other military
    equipment)
harnessed ~ armed for battle; in battle
    array

harrow ~ draw or drag a harrow over (harrow=a frame with spikes or sharp-edged disks, drawn by a horse or tractor and used for breaking up and leveling plowed ground, covering seeds, rooting up weeds

harrows ~ frames with spikes/sharp-edged disks, drawn by a horse or tractor and used for breaking up/leveling plowed ground, covering seeds, rooting up weeds

hart ~ male deer (esp a male red deer of five years), stag

harts ~ male deer (esp a male red deer of five years), stags

hast ~ has ~ 1071

haste ~ hurry

hasted ~ hurried

hasten ~ hurry

hastened ~ hurried

hasteneth ~ hastens ~ 1

hasteth ~ hastes: hurries

hasting ~ hurrying

hatcheth ~ hatches ~ 1

hatest ~ hate ~ 6

hateth ~ hates ~ 31

hath ~ has ~ 2263

haunt ~ frequent; visit often

haunt ~ place often visited or much frequented

have ~ *Gk* hold

have gone over ~ *Gk* finish

have pleasure in ~ *Gk* are being pleased with or agree with

have respect ~ show special honor

having men's persons in admiration ~ admiring men's faces (external status)

havock ~ great destruction

hazarded ~ risked

he ~ male

headlong ~ head first

heady ~ impetuous, rash; willful, headstrong, domineering (*Gk* rash, reckless)

healeth ~ heals ~ 4

heapeth ~ heaps ~ 2

heardest ~ heard ~ 12

hearest ~ hear ~ 11

heareth ~ hears ~ 52

hearken ~ listen carefully

hearkened ~ listened carefully

hearkenedst ~ hearkened ~ 1

hearkeneth ~ hearkens ~ 2

heath ~ small shrub (that grows on the heath or open wasteland)

heaviness ~ grief, sorrow; gloom, dejection; distress, anguish, sorrow

heavy ~ sad, sorrowful; i.e. heavy-hearted; burdened with sorrow

hedge ~ hedge, fence, or barrier

heed ~ careful attention; careful notice; close attention; great care

heifer ~ cow that hasn't given birth

heir ~ inheritor

heirs ~ inheritors

held his peace ~ was silent, kept quiet

held their peace ~ were quiet, kept silent

helm ~ ship's wheel that steers the rudder; tiller

helpeth ~ helps ~ 4

helve ~ handle of a tool, esp of an ax or hatchet

hemlock ~ poisonous plant; poison from that plant

hence ~ from this time or place; from here; away; here

henceforth ~ from this time forward; from now on; hereafter

henceforward ~ from this time forward; from now on

hereafter ~ after this, in the future, from now on, later

hereby ~ by this (means)

herein ~ in this; in this (matter, place, etc.); in here

hereof ~ of this

heresies ~ teachings or opinions that differ with established religious beliefs (*Gk* bodies of men following their own tenets: sects, parties; dissensions arising from diversity of opinions and aims)

heresy ~ teaching or opinion that differs with established religious belief

heretick ~ heretic: a person who professes a heresy--an opinion or teaching that differs with established church beliefs (*Gk* schismatic, factious person {one who causes splits, divisions, factions, parties in a group because of differing opinions or teachings}; a follower of false doctrine; heretic)

heretofore ~ up until now; until the present; before this

hereunto ~ to this (alt of here to)

herewith ~ by this method or means; hereby

heritage ~ *Obs* inheritance

hew ~ shape by cutting or chopping; cut, chop

hewed ~ shaped by chopping, cutting, carving; chopped, cut

hewers ~ choppers, cutters

heweth ~ hews: cuts, chops

hewn ~ carved, chopped, cut

hid ~ hidden

hidest ~ hide ~ 5 ~ hides ~ 1

hideth ~ hides ~ 16

highminded ~ *Arc* haughty, arrogant, proud

hin ~ ancient Hebrew liquid measure=1.5 gallons

hind ~ female deer in and after its third year, esp a red deer

hinder ~ *Rare* hind, rear; posterior

hindereth ~ hinders ~ 1

hindermost ~ *Arc* farthest to the rear, last

hindmost ~ farthest back, farthest to the rear, last

hinds ~ female deer in & after the third year, esp red deer

hire ~ wages, payment

hireling ~ someone for hire; mercenary; hired man

hires ~ payment, wages

hirest ~ hire ~ 1

his own self ~ himself

his state ~ i.e. its proper condition

hither ~ here; to or toward this place

hitherto ~ unto this time or place; up to this point; to now; previously

hoar ~ gray or white with age; white, gray, grayish-white (short for hoary)

hoised ~ *Obs* variant of hoisted

hold ~ *Obs* stronghold (*Heb* cellar; *Gk* prison)

hold ~ take, i.e. consider

hold his peace ~ be quiet, keep silent

hold not thy peace ~ be not silent

hold their peace ~ remain silent, be quiet

hold thy peace ~ be quiet

holden ~ held or held by (*Arc* pp of hold): i.e. covered

holdest me for ~ i.e. treat me as holdest ~ hold ~ 6

holdeth ~ holds ~ 9

holpen ~ helped (*Arc* or *Dial* pp of help)

honest ~ honorable, respectable; commendable

honestly ~ *Gk* decently

honesty ~ *Obs* respectability; purity

honour ~ honor ~ 146

honourable ~ honorable ~ 30

honoured ~ honored ~ 9

honourest ~ honour, ~ honor ~ 1

honoureth ~ honours, ~ honors ~ 9

honours ~ honors ~ 1

hopeth ~ hopes ~ 1

horn ~ emblem of glory, strength, and honor

horseleach ~ aquatic blood-sucking worm differing from the common leach in its larger size and in the formation of its jaws

hosen ~ hose, stockings (*Arc* plural of hose) {*Heb* garment, tunic, coat?: meaning is dubious}

host ~ army, hostile force

hough ~ disable{d} by cutting the sinew or tendon of the hock-- the joint in an animal's hind leg corresponding to the human ankle; hamstring (hough{ed}= *Arc* sp of hock{ed})

houghed ~ disabled by cutting the sinew or tendon of the hock-- the joint in an animal's hind leg corresponding to the human ankle; hamstrung (houghed=*Arc* sp of hocked)

householder ~

householder ~ person who owns or maintains a house alone or as head of the household or family; i.e. lord of the manor; owner or master of a house

how hardly ~ *Rare* with how much difficulty or effort

how many soever ~ however many

howbeit ~ *Arc* nevertheless, be that as it may; however

howsoever ~ however (emphatic)

humbledst ~ humbled ~ 1

humbleth ~ humbles ~ 7

hungerbitten ~ bitten or pinched with hunger; starved, famished

hungered ~ was hungry

huntest ~ hunt ~ 2

hunteth ~ hunts ~ 1

hurleth ~ hurls ~ 1

hurt ~ harm; injury (of tempest-caused violence)

husbandman ~ *Arc* farmer

husbandmen ~ *Arc* farmers

husbandry ~ farming; *Gk* cultivated field, tillage

hypocrisy ~ pretending to be what one is not

hypocrite ~ one who pretends to be better than he is

hypocrites ~ ones pretending to be better than they are; pretenders

idle ~ worthless, useless; *Gk* lazy

idols ~ false gods

ignominy ~ dishonor, disgrace, shame

ill savour ~ bad savor: bad taste or smell

ill ~ evil, bad; badly, poorly

ill favoured ~ bad looking

illuminated ~ enlightened

imagery ~ images collectively (*Heb* carved figures, idols)

imaginations ~ foolish notions; evil plans

imagineth ~ imagines ~ 1
immutability ~ unchangeableness
immutable ~ unchangeable; never changing or varying; unalterable; fixed
impart ~ give
impediment ~ defect, obstruction
impenitent ~ unrepentant
imperious ~ domineering, overbearing, dominant; arrogant
implacable ~ unappeasable, irreconcilable; relentless
implead ~ sue in a court of justice, arraign; accuse; bring charges against
importunity ~ troublesome persistence in insisting or demanding
impotent ~ not powerful, helpless, weak
impudent ~ shamelessly bold or disrespectful, insolent; *Obs* immodest, shameless
impute ~ credit(s)
imputed ~ credited
imputed ~ credited, counted
imputeth ~ imputes: ascribes, credits
imputing ~ crediting, counting
in time past ~ *Gk* once, formerly
in ~ i.e. in the
in ~ i.e. treat . . . As an
in respect of ~ *Obs* in comparison with
in the ear ~ i.e. ripening, forming ears
inasmuch as ~ seeing that, since, because; to the extent that
incensed ~ angry
incline ~ bow or bend down
inclined ~ bent over, stooped down
inclineth ~ inclines ~ 1

incontinency ~ inability to contain or restrain oneself; lack of self-control
incontinent ~ unable to contain or restrain oneself; unrestrained; uncontrolled
increasest ~ increase ~ 1
increaseth ~ increases ~ 15
indeed ~ truly, really, in reality
indignation ~ wrath, anger
inditing ~ *Obs* uttering, suggesting, or inspiring a form of words which is to be repeated or written down; dictating; *Arc* expressing or describing in prose or verse; putting in writing, composing, writing
infallible ~ dependable, reliable, certain
infamy ~ shame, disgrace, reproach, very bad reputation
infidel ~ non-believer; one who is unfaithful or unbelieving toward faith or duty
infirmities ~ weaknesses
infirmity ~ *Gk* weakness
infolding ~ enfolding (variant): wrapping up in folds, enveloping, enclosing
inhabitest ~ inhabit ~ 1
inhabiteth ~ inhabits ~ 2
inheriteth ~ inherits ~ 1
iniquity ~ lawlessness
iniquity ~ injustice
injurious ~ likely to cause injury; harmful; offensive or abusive; slanderous or libelous (*Gk* insolent; one who, uplifted with pride, either heaps insulting language upon others or does them some shameful act of wrong)

inkhorn ~ small container made of horn or other material formerly used to hold ink; inkwell

innumerable multitude ~ uncountable crowd

innumerable ~ uncountable

inordinate affection ~ uncontrolled passions

inordinate ~ excessive, unrestrained

inquisition ~ investigation, examination, inquiry

insomuch ~ to such a degree or extent; in as much; so; with that

instant ~ urgent, insistent, persistent; earnest

instantly ~ *Arc* urgently, insistently, persistently; earnestly

insurrection ~ rebellion, revolt

intelligence ~ knowledge, understanding, insight; information

intendest ~ intend ~ 1

intent ~ purpose, intention

intents ~ intentions, purposes

intermeddle ~ *Obs* concern himself with (*Heb* share, have fellowship with)

intermeddleth ~ *Arc* of intermeddles: gets mixed-up with; *Obs* concerns himself with

intreat ~ *Arc* variant of entreat: beg, beseech, implore

intreated ~ *Arc* sp entreated: earnestly asked, begged, implored; i.e. heard and answered; plead with

intruding ~ entering (without permission)

inventions ~ plans, schemes, designs, devices, contrivances

inward ~ *Obs* intimate, close, confidential: belonging to the inner circle of one's acquaintances or friends

inwards ~ entrails, guts, inner or interior organs

isle ~ island, esp a small one; *Heb* coast, shore, region, island

isles ~ coasts, shores, regions, islands

issue ~ flow out, discharge; spring out

issue ~ outflow: offspring, children

issued ~ flowed

issues ~ outflowings

jacinth ~ reddish-orange gemstone

jasper ~ variously colored precious stone: either purple, blue, green, or brass; clear jasper

jeoparded ~ endangered, risked (*rare* form of jeopardized)

jeopardy ~ risk of loss, harm, peril, death, or injury; great danger

Jesus ~ i.e. Joshua (*Heb* equivalent of Jesus)

Jewry ~ *Obs* name for Judea

joinings ~ *Heb* clamps, fittings, bindings, joints

Jonas ~ Jonah ~ 12

jot ~ smallest letter of the Hebrew alphabet; little bit of something

joyed we ~ we rejoiced

jubile ~ time of rejoicing or celebration

judgest ~ judge ~ 8

judgeth ~judges: examines, discerns

judgment ~ justice

just ~ righteous; i.e. to be just

justified ~ *Gk* shown or declared righteous (by); *Obs* acknowledged as true or genuine

justifieth ~ justifies ~ 4

justify ~ declare(s) righteous

justle ~ variant of jostle: bump, or push (as in a crowd)

keep under ~ *Gk* beat black & blue; discipline by hardships

keep ~ guard(s), protect(s)

keeper of the prison ~ *Gk* jailer or keeper of a prison

keeper ~ guardian, protector; caretaker; watchman, gamekeeper

keepers ~ guards

keepest ~ keep ~ 4

keepeth ~ guards, protects

keepeth ~ keeps: guards

kept holyday ~ held a religious festival or feast

kept ~ guarded, protected; celebrated; i.e. stayed in

kerchiefs ~ cloths used to cover women's heads (*Heb* veils)

kernels ~ seeds contained within any fruit

kid ~ baby or young goat (prepared for a meal)

kids ~ young or baby goats

kill ~ *Heb* murder

killedst ~ killed ~ 2

killest ~ kill ~ 2

killeth ~ kills ~ 23

kin ~ kinfolk, relatives, family

kindle ~ stir up; ignite; catch fire

kindleth ~ kindles ~ 3

kindred ~ family

kindreds ~ families, tribes

kine ~ cows, cattle

kinsfolk ~ *Obs* kinfolk: family, relatives

kinsfolks ~ kinfolk: relatives

kinsman ~ relative (male)

kinsmen ~ relatives (male)

kinswoman ~ female relative

knew ~ recognized

knew ~ knew (sexually)

knewest ~ knew ~ 10

knit ~ tied; bound, knotted

knocketh ~ knocks ~ 4

knop ~ knob; esp a knob-like ornament

knops ~ knobs; esp knob-like ornaments: knobs= rounded lumps or protuberances

know the uttermost ~ *Gk* know accurately or ascertain exactly

know ~ know (sexually)

knowest ~ know ~ 89

knoweth ~ knows ~ 104

known ~ known (sexually)

labour ~ labor ~ 88

laboured ~ labored ~ 19

labourer ~ laborer ~ 2

labourers ~ laborers ~ 9

laboureth ~ labours, ~ labors ~ 5

labouring ~ laboring ~ 4

labours ~ labors ~ 13

lack of service ~ *Gk* deficiency or poverty of charitable giving

lackest ~ lack ~ 2

lacketh ~ lacks ~ 5

lade ~ load, burden down

laded ~ loaded, burdened down

laden ~ loaded, burdened down (Rare)

ladeth ~ lades: loads, burdens down (Rare)

lading ~ loading, burdening; load, burden (Rare)

laid to their charge ~ credited to them

laid ~ added: joined, gathered; taken

laid ~ placed in a resting position

laidst ~ laid ~ 1

lament ~ mourn, grieve; feel deep sorrow or express it by weeping or wailing

lamentation ~ wailing, weeping, mourning

lance ~ spear, javelin

lancets ~ small spears, javelins; darts

languish ~ pine away, grown weak

languished ~ became weak; drooped

languisheth ~ languishes: loses vigor or vitality; droops; wastes away

languishing ~ sickness, weakness

lanterns ~ encased torches

lappeth ~ laps ~ 2

lapwing ~ a bird so named because of its irregular flight and spectacular aerial displays

large ~ i.e. a large sum of

lasciviousness ~ lustfulness, licentiousness, lewdness, wantonness

latchet ~ *Arc* strap/ lace for fastening a sandal/ shoe to foot

lately ~ recently

latter ~ last

laud ~ extol, praise, magnify

laugh them to scorn ~ treat them with extreme, often indignant, contempt or utter disdain

laugh me to scorn ~ treat me with extreme, often indignant, contempt or utter disdain

laughed us to scorn ~ treated us with extreme, often indignant, contempt or utter disdain

laughed to scorn ~ treated with extreme, often indignant, contempt or utter disdain

laughed them to scorn ~ treated them with extreme, often indignant, contempt or utter disdain

laughed him to scorn ~ treated him with extreme, often indignant, contempt or utter disdain

laughed thee to scorn ~ treated thee with extreme, often indignant, contempt or utter disdain

laugheth ~ laughs ~ 1

laver ~ basin, bowl, or other vessel for washing

lavers ~ basins, bowls, or other vessels for washing

lay up ~ treasure up

lay sore ~ *Arc* put great pressure

lay hold on ~ take hold of

layedst ~ layed ~ 1

layest ~ lay ~ 2

layeth ~ lays ~ 18

leadest ~ lead ~ 1

leadeth ~ leads ~ 14

league ~ agreement, alliance(for mutual protection)

leaneth ~ leans ~ 2

leanfleshed ~ lean + fleshed: thin, gaunt, lean

leasing ~ *Obs* lying, falsehood, deceit

least ~ smallest

leave ~ permission

leave caring for ~ stop worrying about

leaven ~ substance used to make bread rise: fermented dough or yeast

leavened ~ with leaven or yeast

leaveneth ~ leavens ~ 2

leaveth ~ leaves ~ 6

leddest ~ led ~ 5

lees ~ dregs, sediment

left off to build ~ i.e. stopped building

left off ~ i.e. stopped

left communing ~ i.e. stopped talking

left ~ stopped, quit

leftest ~ left ~ 1

legion ~ Roman legion: 3,000-6,000 foot soldiers

legions ~ each Roman legion ranged
    from 3,000-6,000 foot soldiers
lendeth ~ lends ~ 4
lent ~ *Rare* gave, imparted
lentiles ~ lentils ~ 4
let **it** **forth** ~ leased, or rented it out
let ~ rented, leased
let ~ rent
let ~ *Arc* hindered
let ~ *Arc* hinder, prevent, obstruct,
    restrain
letters ~ letters: literature, writings,
    learning
lettest ~ let ~ 3
letteth ~ lets: *Arc* hinders, prevents,
    obstructs, restrains
leviathan ~ sea monster (perhaps an
    extinct dinosaur)
levy **a** **tribute** ~ impose a regular
    obligation of; i.e. collect a tax
    or collection
levy ~ drafted labor force
lewd ~ *Obs* unprincipled, vicious
lewd ~ showing, or intended to incite,
    lust or sexual desire, esp in an
    offensive way; lascivious
lewdness ~ unrestrained lustfulness &
    eroticism; *Obs* viciousness,
    villainy
liberal ~ generous, noble
liberality ~ generosity: i.e. gift
liberally ~ generously, freely
libertines ~ freed slaves
licence ~ license: permission,
    freedom, liberty, opportunity
licketh ~ licks ~ 1
lien ~ *Arc* of lain
liest ~ lie ~ 5
lieth ~ lies/lie ~ 59
lift ~ lifted
liftest ~ lift/lifts ~ 4
lifteth ~ lifts ~ 10

light ~ frivolous, reckless; i.e. small,
    insignificant
light ~ alight, descend, fall
lighted **off** ~ *Dial* alighted: got down
    from or off; dismounted
lighted ~ *Dial* alighted: got down
    from or off; dismounted;
    descended and settled; *Rare*
    came on or upon accidentally
lighten ~ illuminate
lighteneth ~ lightens: shines
lightest ~ light ~ 1
lighteth ~ lights: *Arc* of *Dial* alights:
    Rare comes on or upon
    accidentally i.e. lands on
lighting **down** ~ *Dial* alighting:
    descent
lighting ~ *Dial* alighting: landing
lightly ~ with little motion; gently;
    Rare quickly, speedily; with
    ease
lightly ~ casually, frivolously,
    recklessly; with indifference
    or neglect
lightness ~ recklessness,
    frivolousness; wantonness
lign **aloes** ~ lign-aloes: wood of the
    aloe: yields an aromatic wood
    called eagle wood; contains an
    oil used in perfumes, soaps,
    foods, etc.
ligure ~ precious stone thought to be
    yellow jacinth
like **wise** ~ similar manner or way
like **unto** ~ similar to
like **to** ~ similar to
like ~ similar; same, exact same;
    similarly; even, just; i.e. about
like **passions** ~ similar feelings or
    emotions
like **figure** ~ *Gk* anti-type
liken ~ compare

likened ~ compared

liketh ~ likes: *Arc* pleases

likewise ~ in a similar manner

liking ~ *Arc* (in) condition, health

limiteth ~ limits ~ 1

lingered ~ hesitated, continued to stay

lingereth ~ lingers: delays

lintel ~ horizontal support or crosspiece over door top

liquor ~ juice, liquid

liquors ~ juices or other liquids (*Heb* juices)

listed ~ *Arc* wished, liked, chose

listeth ~ *Arc* wishes, likes, chooses

listeth ~ lists ~ > ~ wills ~ 2

litters ~ enclosed or curtained couches mounted on shafts and used to carry a single passenger; stretchers (*Heb* carrying vehicles; liters; covered wagons)

little space ~ short time, little while

little of stature ~ small of height: i.e. short

little ~ *Gk* for a little (time)

lively ~ vigorous, full of life, living, active

livest ~ live ~ 4

liveth ~ lives ~ 96

living ~ life-support: wealth, goods; means of sustaining life

living ~ i.e. not stagnant, but fresh springing

loadeth ~ loads ~ 1

loathe ~ abhor, detest, feel intense dislike, disgust, or hatred for

loatheth ~ loathes: abhors, detests, feels intense dislike, disgust, or hatred for

loathsome ~ abhorrent, detestable, disgusting, nauseating

lodge ~ small (servant) house

lodge ~ rest, live, or stay for a time; stay as a guest; pass the night

lodged ~ temporarily housed or stayed; rested, stayed for a while; temporarily staying

lodgest ~ lodge ~ 1

lodgeth ~ lodges: temporarily stays

lodging ~ place to stay; (temporary) living quarters

loft ~ story

loins ~ the hips or lower abdomen

long forbearing ~ i.e. self-restraint

long ~ i.e. for a long

longedst ~ longed ~ 1

longeth ~ longs ~ 4

look ye out ~ find, select

look out ~ i.e. find

lookest ~ look ~ 2

looketh ~ looks ~ 33

looking glass ~ mirror

loose ~ untie, release; *Poetic* break

loosed ~ loosened; released

looseth ~ looses ~ 2

loosing ~ untying, releasing

lop ~ trim

lord ~ master

lordly ~ noble, suitable for a lord; regal

loseth ~ loses ~ 1

lot ~ object used to randomly decide; i.e. casting lots to randomly choose

lot ~ randomly determined task; allotment or allotted portion (randomly selected)

lothe ~ loathe: feel intense dislike, disgust, hatred for; detest, hate

lotheth ~ loathes: despises, hates

lothing ~ loathing: intense disgust

lots ~ objects used to make random decisions

lovedst ~ loved ~ 2

lovest ~ love ~ 12
loveth ~ loves ~ 65
loweth ~ lows ~ 1
lowring ~ lowering: dark-clouded;
    overcast, gloomy
lucre ~ illicit, dishonorable, or
    unlawful gain or advantage
lunatick ~ *Arc* for lunatic: moon-
    struck, insane (epileptic ??)
lust ~ strong desire, craving
lust ~ strongly desire or crave
lusted after ~ craved
lusteth ~ lusts: strongly desires
lusts of ~ cravings or strong desires
    for
lusts ~ strong or intense desires,
    cravings
lusty ~ vigorous, lively, robust
mad upon ~ i.e. insane, crazy about
mad ~ insane, crazy; enraged, angry
made ready to our hand ~ *Gk*
    already prepared
made ready ~ prepared
made of none effect ~ *Gk* made vain,
    useless; deprived of force,
    influence, or power;
    inactivated; annulled
made manifest ~ clearly or plainly
    revealed or shown
made insurrection ~ revolted
made haste ~ hurried
made ~ i.e. acted
madest ~ made ~ 10
madness ~ insanity
magnifical ~ *Obs* magnificent:
    renowned, glorious, stately
magnified ~ *Arc* glorified, praised
maid ~ *Poetic* girl or young
    unmarried woman; *Obs* virgin;
    girl or woman servant
maiden ~ *Obs* virgin; young,
    unmarried woman

mail ~ flexible body armor composed
    of small overlapping metal
    rings, loops of chain, or scales
maimed ~ those who are missing an
    important body part like an
    arm, hand, leg, foot, eye, or
    ear
maintainest ~ maintain ~ 1
maintenance ~ sustenance, means of
    support
majesty ~ great splendor
make ready ~ prepare
make merchandise of you ~ *Gk* use
    you for gain
make haste ~ hurry
make fat ~ *Heb* make strong, brace
    up, invigorate
makest ~ make ~ 26
maketh ~ makes ~ 126
malefactor ~ evil doer, criminal
malefactors ~ evil doers, criminals
malice ~ desire to harm others or to
    see others suffer; extreme ill
    will or spite
maliciousness ~ evil
malignity ~ deep-rooted or intense ill-
    will/hatred; great malice
mallows ~ plants that grow in salt
    marshes
mammon ~ Aramaic word for riches:
    riches, money, wealth;
    sometimes personified as a
    false god or an object of
    worship; often regarded as an
    evil influence
man ~ male
man ~ human (*Gk* anthrOpos)
mandrakes ~ poisonous plants of the
    nightshade family formerly
    used in medicine for their
    narcotic and emetic prop-
    erties (*Heb* mandrakes, love-
    apples: thought to excite

sexual desire or encourage procreation)

manifest ~ clearly reveal

manifest ~ plain, clear, obvious,evident; revealed, made known

manifestation ~ revealing: _Gk_ unveiling, disclosure

manifested forth ~ clearly or plainly revealed

manifested ~ clearly revealed; made plain; made visible, clear, known

manifestly ~ clearly

manifold temptations ~ various testings

manifold ~ much (of various kinds); many, numerous, abundant; multi-faceted; multi-colored

mankind ~ human males in general; the male sex

manner ~ kind; kinds; kinds of

manners ~ character, behavior

mansions ~ resting, abiding, or dwelling places

manslayers ~ _Gk_ man-murderers

mantle ~ loose, sleeveless cloak or cape of varying lengths

mantles ~ loose, sleeveless cloaks or capes of varying lengths

mar ~ disfigure, spoil; damage

Maranatha ~ _Gk_ our Lord comes or will come

marchedst ~ marched ~ 1

marishes ~ marshes, swamps, bogs, or other wetlands

mark ~ target

mark ~ note, observe

markest ~ mark ~ 1

marketh ~ marks ~ 3

marred ~ injured or damaged so as to make imperfect, less

attractive: disfigured, spoiled, ruined

marrieth ~ marries ~ 4

mart ~ market place, trading center

marvel ~ wonder

marvelled ~ marveled: wondered

marvellous ~ marvelous: wonderful, amazing

marvellously ~ marvelously

maschil ~ _Heb_ poem, song or poem of contemplation

master ~ _Gk_ sailing master, helmsman

master ~ teacher, rabbi; owner; lord, head

masteries ~ competition-victories

masters ~ i.e. (authoritative) teachers, esp of Bible

mastery ~ rule, control; victory in competition

matrix ~ womb

matter ~ _Obs_ forest, wood, timber

mattock ~ tool used for loosening hard ground or cutting roots; pickax, hoe, plowshare

mattocks ~ tools used for loosening hard ground or cutting roots; pickaxes, hoes, plowshares

maul ~ very heavy hammer, club, or mallet

maw ~ stomach of an animal, esp the fourth stomach of a cud-chewing animal

mayest ~ may ~ 114

me thinketh ~ I think

mean ~ common, obscure, insignificant, low

meanest ~ mean ~ 4

meaneth ~ means ~ 8

measure ~ _Gk_ beyond measure: greatly

meat ~ _Arc_ food

meats ~ foods

meddleth ~ meddles ~ 1

meet ~ *Rare* proper, fitting, suitable, becoming

meetest ~ fittest, best-qualified

meetest ~ meet ~ 1

meeteth ~ meets ~ 3

melteth ~ melts ~ 7

member ~ body part

members ~ body part(s)

men of low estate ~ *Gk* the ones of lowly condition

men ~ male

merchandise ~ trade: buying & selling; wares

mess ~ portion, share, ration, allotment of food

messes ~ portions, shares, rations, allotments of food

mete ~ *Arc* measure

meted ~ *Arc* measured

meteyard ~ *Arc* measurement (standard of measurement)

midst ~ middle

mightest ~ might ~ 19

milch ~ *Arc* milk-giving

mill ~ place where grain is ground into flour or meal; device that grinds grain

millet ~ a cereal grass whose small grain is used for food in Europe and Asia

millstone ~ either of a pair of large flat stones between which grain or other substances are ground

mincing ~ walking with little steps; affecting daintiness

mind ~ think about, seek

mind ~ way of thinking, mind-set; opinion; i.e. will

minded ~ inclined, disposed, resolved, determined

mindful of ~ remembering

minding ~ intending

mingled ~ mixed, blended, combined

minish ~ *Arc* make or become less; diminish

minished ~ *Arc* made less; diminished

minister unto ~ serve, assist, help with

minister ~ give aid, assistance, help; provide, serve, assist; i.e. promote; *Arc* provide, supply

minister ~ servant, assistant, helper, attendant; *Gk* priest-like servant

minister for ~ serve, assist, help

minister to ~ serve, assist, help

ministered unto him of their substance ~ *Gk* were helping him from their own resources

ministered ~ furnished, supplied

ministered unto ~ served, helped, assisted

ministereth ~ ministers: provides

ministers ~ servants

ministration ~ service, ministry

ministry ~ priestly service

minstrel ~ *Poetic* musician (*Heb* player of a stringed instrument)

minstrels ~ Old *Poetic* musicians (*Gk* flute players)

mire ~ deep mud; wet, soggy ground; bog

mirth ~ joyfulness, merriment, laughter

mischief ~ injury, harm, damage esp done by a person; action or conduct that causes damage or trouble

mischievous ~ harmful, injurious

miserably ~ painfully, wretchedly

mite ~ small brass coin worth about 1/5 of a cent

mites ~ small brass coins each worth about 1/5 of a cent

mitre ~ Brit sp of miter: cap, headband, turban; headdress or other ceremonial headwear

moan ~ lament; mourn over; show grief or pity over

mockest ~ mock ~ 1

mocketh ~ mocks ~ 5

moderation ~ *Gk* gentleness, mildness, fairness

mollified ~ softened, soothed, pacified, made tender

molten ~ formed by melting & casting in mold; metal melted then poured into a mold

more part ~ majority

more a great deal ~ *Gk* much more

more ~ more in number or importance

morrow ~ next day, day following; *Arc* next day, next morning

mortify ~ destroy the vitality or vigor of (*Gk* destroy, kill)

mote ~ speck of dirt or dust; splinter, chip of wood

mount ~ *Obs* raised fortification

mounts ~ *Obs* raised fortifications

mourneth ~ mourns ~ 11

moved with ~ motivated by

moved ~ carried along

moved sedition ~ *Obs* made a revolt or rebellion

movedst ~ moved ~ 1

moveth ~ moves ~ 8

much speaking ~ i.e. many words

much ~ many; very

mufflers ~ kerchiefs, scarves (*Heb* probably veils)

multipliedst ~ multiplied ~ 1

multiplieth ~ multiplies ~ 3

multitude ~ crowd, masses of people; number

multitudes ~ crowds, masses of people

munition ~ *Arc* fortification, stronghold; bulwark, siege-works

munitions ~ *Arc* fortifications, strongholds

murmur ~ grumble, mutter, or mumble complaints

murmured ~ grumbled; complained by muttering; muttered complaints

murmurers ~ grumblers

murmuring ~ grumbling, muttering of complaints; complainings

murmurings ~ muttered or mumbled complaints; grumblings, complainings

murrain ~ any of various infectious cattle-diseases; *Arc* plague, pestilence

muse ~ meditate, think deeply and at length

mused ~ meditated, thought deeply and at length

musick ~ music

musing ~ meditating, thinking deeply and at length

mustered ~ gathered, summoned (for military duty)

mustereth ~ musters: gathers (an army)

nameth ~ names ~ 1

napkin ~ any small cloth or towel; Brit handkerchief (*Gk* handkerchief; a cloth for wiping perspiration from the face and for cleaning the nose and also used in swathing the head of a corpse)

nativity ~ birth, esp of place, time, or conditions

naturally ~ in a natural manner; by nature, innately; *Gk* genuinely, faithfully, sincerely

naught ~ *Obs* worthless, useless (alt sp of nought--nothing)

naughtiness ~ *Obs* wickedness, viciousness, depravity

naughty ~ *Obs* bad, evil

naves ~ wheel-hubs

nay ~ no

necromancer ~ one who claims to foretell the future by alleged communication with the dead; a practicer of black magic, sorcery

needest ~ need ~ 1

needeth ~ needs ~ 6

needlework ~ embroidery, fancywork--ornamental work

needs be ~ of necessity be, necessarily be (i.e. act like)

needs ~ of necessity, necessarily

neesings ~ sneezings, sneezes (*Arc* sp); sneezing

neighbour ~ neighbor ~ 107

neighbours ~ neighbors ~ 21

neighbours' ~ neighbors' ~ 1

neighbour's ~ neighbor's ~ 28

neighed ~ whinnied (made the characteristic horse sound)

neighing ~ whinnying (the characteristic sound of a horse)

neighings ~ whinnyings (the characteristic sounds of a horse)

nephews ~ *Obs* descendants, grandsons (*Heb* progeny, posterity; *Gk* grandchildren, offspring, descendants)

net ~ network or grate

nether ~ lower

nethermost ~ lowest

nigh ~ *Dialect* near; *Dialect* nearly, almost

nigh at hand ~ *Dialect* near+close by; *Gk* near

nigh ~ near100-

nitre ~ Brit sp of niter--sodium nitrate, a cleansing agent (*Heb* natron, nitre, soda, carbonate of soda)

no wise ~ no way

no brawlers ~ free from noisy fights or quarrels

no striker ~ not addicted to striking or hitting

Noe ~ Noah ~ 5

noised abroad ~ rumored, reported far and wide

noised ~ rumored, reported

noisome ~ harmful, injurious to health

none occasion ~ no cause

none ~ no; no one

noontide ~ noon time, noon, midday

notable ~ notorious, infamous; outstanding, remarkable; *Gk* conspicuous

nothing laid to his charge ~ *Gk* not one accusation

notwithstanding ~ greet

nought ~ nothing (var of naught)

nought ~ *Gk* utterly despised, treated with contempt

nourisheth ~ nourishes ~ 1

novice ~ new convert

now of a long time ~ *Gk* from long ago

numberest ~ number ~ 3

nurture ~ the act or process of raising or promoting the development of: training, educating, fostering, etc. (*Gk* the whole training and education of children {which relates to the cultivation of mind and morals, and employs for this purpose now commands and admonitions, now reproof and punishment; It also includes the training and care of the body.})

obeisance ~ expression of submission, often involving a bow

obeyedst ~ obeyed ~ 2

obeyeth ~ obeys ~ 3

oblation ~ sacrifice or offering

oblations ~ sacrifices or offerings

observation ~ kjv margin: outward show

observest ~ observe ~ 1

observeth ~ observes ~ 1

obtaineth ~ obtains ~ 2

occasion ~ incident; cause; reason; opportunity

occupied ~ traded, bartered, marketed

occupied ~ used

occupiers ~ *Arc* marketers, traders, barterers, exchangers

occupieth ~ occupies: fills

occupy ~ *Arc* market, trade, barter, exchange; i.e. make a profit (with)

occurrent ~ *Arc* occurrence, event, action, incident

odd ~ left over, irregular

odious ~ offensive, disgusting, detestable, repugnant; arousing or deserving hatred or loathing

odour ~ odor ~ 2

odours ~ fragrances

odours ~ odors: *Arc* perfume, incense; sweet smells

of the ranges ~ from the rows, ranks (of soldiers)

of late ~ lately

of above ~ by more than

of his own accord ~ automatically (*Gk* automatos)

of ~ i.e. out of, from; i.e. by; i.e. on; i.e. for a

of ~ for; at; with; by; on; *Gk* according to; *Gk* by

of a child ~ *Gk* from childhood

of a long season ~ for a long time

of a surety ~ i.e. certainly

of a truth ~ truly

offence ~ *Gk* cause of stumbling

offend thee ~ cause (thee) to stumble

offend ~ cause(s) to stumble; *Gk* scandalize(s)

offended ~ caused to stumble; *Gk* scandalized; *Gk* sinned (in)

offereth ~ offers ~ 15

offscouring ~ what is scoured off: filth; refuse cleaned off and thrown away

oft ~ Literary variant of often

oftener ~ more frequently, often

oftentimes ~ *Poetic* of often: often, frequently

ofttimes ~ *Poetic* of often: often, frequently

oil olive ~ i.e. olive oil

oiled ~ moistened with or containing oil

omer ~ Hebrew unit of dry measure c. 1/10 of an ephah

omnipotent ~ all powerful, having unlimited power or authority

on usury ~ at (excessively high) interest

on this wise ~ in this way

on a smoke ~ i.e. covered with smoke

on ~ in

one cubit ~ c. 18 inches

one born out of due time ~ a miscarriage

only begotten ~ *Gk* i.e. uniquely-related (one): monO-genAs

onycha ~ the operculum (the horny plate serving to close the shell when the animal is retracted) of a marine mollusk which emits a penetrating aroma when burned

openest ~ open ~ 2

openeth ~ opens ~ 21

opening ~ (of the mind)

operation ~ work, working

operations ~ works, workings

opposest ~ oppose ~ 1

opposeth ~ opposes ~ 1

oppresseth ~ oppresses ~ 5

or ever ~ before

oracle ~ holy of holies in the Jewish tabernacle & temple

oracles ~ words or utterances of God

oration ~ formal speech

orator ~ eloquent public speaker

ordaineth ~ ordains ~ 1

order ~ arrangement, instructions

ordereth ~ orders ~ 1

ordinance ~ *Gk* institution; *Arc* governmental system

ordinances ~ prescribed practices; traditions

Osee ~ Hosea

osprey ~ a large black and white diving bird that feeds mainly on fish (Heb. Perhaps an extinct bird, meaning uncertain)

ossifrage ~ Lit. "bone-breaker": vulture (*Arc* of Osprey)

ouches ~ brooches or clasps; settings for precious stones

ought ~ anything

oughtest ~ ought ~ 4

out of ~ beyond, i.e. before (their)

out ~ spy, catch sight of; see

outgoings ~ extremities, outer limits, borders

outlandish ~ *Arc* foreign, alien

outmost ~ outermost, most remote

outwent ~ went before, went ahead, preceded

over much ~ too much

over ~ upon

over against ~ on the other side of, opposite to; next to, before; near; in front of; toward

overcharge ~ overload, overburden

overcharged ~ overloaded, overburdened; filled too full

overcometh ~ overcomes ~ 11

overdrive ~ severely drive

overfloweth ~ overflows ~ 1

overlaid ~ lay on top of

overlived ~ outlived, survived (*Obs*)

overmuch ~ too much

overpass ~ pass over

overpast ~ passed over

overplus ~ surplus

overran ~ *Arc* outran

overrunning ~ i.e. overwhelming

overspread ~ scattered, dispersed

overtaketh ~ overtakes ~ 1

overthroweth ~ overthrows ~ 5

overturneth ~ overturns ~ 3

owest ~ owe ~ 4

oweth ~ owes ~ 1

owneth ~ owns ~ 2

pacifieth ~ pacifies ~ 2

paddle ~ small spade or trowel

painful ~ *Arc* laborious, difficult, painstaking

paintedst ~ painted ~ 1

pair of balances ~ pair of scales (for weighing by balancing)

palestina ~ i.e. Palestine

palmerworm ~ migratory caterpillar

palms ~ palm branches

palsies ~ paralysis of any voluntary muscles as a result of some disorder to nervous system, sometimes accompanied by involuntary tremors

palsy ~ paralysis of any voluntary muscles as a result of some disorder to the nervous system, sometimes accompanied with involuntary tremors

pangs ~ sudden, sharp, and brief pains--physical or emo-tional; spasms of distress

panteth ~ pants ~ 3

paps ~ *Arc* nipples or teats (*Heb* breasts; *Gk* breasts)

paramours ~ lovers, esp the illicit sexual partners of a married man or woman

parched ~ dried up with heat; hot and dry; dried, roasted

parchments ~ i.e. scrolls made of animal skins

pardoneth ~ pardons ~ 1

parlour ~ reception room, formal sitting room: alt spell parlor

parlour ~ parlor ~ 5

parlours ~ reception rooms, formal sitting rooms: alt spell parlors)

parlours ~ parlors ~ 1

part ~ side or party (in a conflict)

part ~ divide

partakest ~ partake ~ 1

parted ~ divided into parts; separated, divided

parteth ~ parts ~ 3

particularly ~ specifically

partition ~ separation, division

passages ~ fords

passedst ~ passed ~ 1

passest ~ pass ~ 5

passeth ~ passes: surpasses; *Gk* surpasses

passion ~ suffering or agony

passover ~ *Gk* Passover lamb

past feeling ~ *Gk* callous; insensible to pain

pastors ~ shepherds

pate ~ head, esp the top or crown of the head

patriarch ~ father & ruler of a family or tribe

patrimony ~ inheritance from one's father or ancestors

pavilion ~ large tent, usually with a peaked top

pavilions ~ large tents with a peaked top

paweth ~ paws ~ 1

payed ~ paid ~ 2

payeth ~ pays ~ 1

peculiar ~ special, particular; belonging exclusively

pence ~ *Gk* denarius--Roman silver coin: each equal to c. a day's labor

penny ~ *Gk* denarius--a Roman silver coin: equal to c. a day's labor

pennyworth ~ *Gk* denarius--Roman silver coins: each equal to c. a day's labor

pentecost ~ the second of the three great Jewish feasts, cele-brated at Jerusalem yearly, the seventh week after the Passover, in grateful recognition of the completed harvest; fiftieth day after Passover

penury ~ lack of money, property, or necessities; extreme poverty; destitution

peradventure ~ *Arc* perhaps, possibly; by chance
perceivest ~ perceive ~ 2
perceiveth ~ perceives ~ 3
perdition ~ damnation, utter ruin, destruction
performeth ~ performs ~ 4
peril ~ danger
perilous ~ dangerous
perils ~ dangers
perish ~ be destroyed
perisheth ~ perishes ~ 9
perjured persons ~ ones who lie under oath
pernicious ~ destructive, hurtful, *Rare* wicked
perpetual ~ perpetually: permanently, without interruption
perplexed ~ puzzled, confused, doubtful
perplexity ~ uncertainty, confusion, bewilderment
persecutest ~ persecute ~ 6
perseverance ~ continued, patient effort; persistence
persuadest ~ persuade ~ 1
persuadeth ~ persuades ~ 2
pertaineth ~ pertains ~ 7
perverse ~ wicked; stubbornly contrary, obstinate; corrupt(ed); deviated from what is right; twisted away from the good
perverseness ~ persistence in error or fault; stubbornness; deviation from what is right and good
pervert ~ twist, distort; corrupt
perverteth ~ perverts ~ 5
pestilence ~ infectious, deadly disease; plague
pestilences ~ deadly contagious diseases
pestilent ~ dangerous, troublesome

petition ~ solemn request to superior
phylacteries ~ boxes for Scripture
pictures ~ images carved in relief
pierceth ~ pierces ~ 1
piety ~ affectionate loyalty & respect
pilled ~ peeled (British Dialect)
pine ~ waste
pineth ~ pines: wastes
pinnacle ~ high point, peak
pipe ~ flute, pan-pipe
piped unto ~ played the flute for
piped ~ played the flute or pan-pipe
pipers ~ flute players
pipes ~ flutes
piss ~ urine (formerly acceptable, now Vulgar)
pisseth ~ urinates (once acceptable; now Vulgar)
pitch ~ black, sticky waterproofing material; water-proofing sealer
pitch ~ smear or cover with pitch, tar
pitieth ~ pities ~ 3
pitiful ~ *Arc* full of pity or compassion; merciful
place ~ space, room; [your] place; i.e. ground
plague ~ affliction, calamity
plagues ~ afflictions or calamities
plaiting ~ braiding, folding, weaving (pleating)
plantedst ~ planted ~ 2
planteth ~ plants ~ 5
plat ~ small plot or portion of land
platted ~ braided, weaved, or woven
play ~ sport; *Obs* engage in sexual activity
playedst ~ played ~ 2
playeth ~ plays ~ 1
pleadeth ~ pleads ~ 3
pleaseth ~ pleases ~ 6

pledge ~ object given to secure a debt; security, down-payment; collateral

pledges ~ objects that guarantee a promise

plenteous ~ plentiful

plotteth ~ plots ~ 1

ploweth ~ plows ~ 1

plowshares ~ cutting blade of moldboard plows

pluck ~ snatch, take by violence

plucked asunder ~ pulled apart or into pieces or parts

plucketh ~ plucks ~ 1

pluckt ~ plucked ~ 1

plummet ~ plumb bob`

poll ~ trim, clip, cut-off (the hair of)

polled ~ (*Arc*) shaved, cut the hair (on the head)

polls ~ heads; head counts--census

polluted ~ profaned, defiled, desecrated

pommels ~ rounded kn*obs* (*Heb* bowl-shaped portions of the capitals of temple pillars)

pomp ~ stately or showy display

pondered ~ thought deeply about

pondereth ~ ponders ~ 3

porter ~ door or gate keeper

porters ~ door or gate keepers

possessest ~ possess ~ 1

possesseth ~ possesses ~ 2

possessions ~ fields

post ~ runner, courier

posts ~ runners, couriers

potentate ~ someone having great power: sovereign, ruler, king, dictator

potsherd ~ fragment or broken piece of pottery

pottage ~ contents of a pot: stew, soup, porridge

pound ~ originally a pound weight of silver: OT 1 pound=300 shekels; NT 100 pounds=1 talent, 1 pound=10.33 oz or 300 g

pouredst ~ poured ~ 1

poureth ~ pours ~ 11

pourtray ~ portray: display

pourtrayed ~ portrayed: pictured

power ~ ability; *Gk* authority: symbol or sign of authority

powers ~ authorities

praiseth ~ praises ~ 1

prating ~ foolish, idle, boastful, excessive, or vain talking

pray ~ *Rare* earnestly ask or beg, implore, beseech

prayed ~ asked, begged

prayest ~ pray ~ 2

prayeth ~ prays ~ 7

praying ~ begging

preachest ~ preach ~ 1

preacheth ~ preaches ~ 3

predestinate ~ predetermine,

predestinated ~ decreed beforehand; foreordained

preparedst ~ prepared ~ 1

preparest ~ prepare ~ 3

prepareth ~ prepares ~ 3

presbytery ~ assembly of elders

preservest ~ preserve ~ 2

preserveth ~ preserves ~ 8

press ~ *Arc* crowd, throng

pressed upon ~ i.e. plead with, strongly urged

presseth ~ presses ~ 2

pressfat ~ wine-press, wine vat

presumptuous sins ~ sins of arrogance or overconfidence

presumptuous ~ arrogant, overconfident

presumptuously ~ boldly, arrogantly; overconfidently; insolently, defiantly

pretence ~ false show or claim; pretext

prevailed ~ i.e. overwhelmed

prevailest ~ prevail ~ 1

prevaileth ~ prevails

prevent ~ *Obs* come or go before; precede, anticipate

prevented ~ *Obs* come or gone before; preceded, anticipated

preventest ~ prevent: *Obs* come or go before; precede, anticipate

prey ~ plunder; hunt or kill another animal; victimize

prey ~ plunder; animal hunted or killed by another animal; victim; *Heb* plunder; gift, prize

pricks ~ *Arc* any of various pointed objects as thorns, goads, etc

principal ~ most important; chief, main; head

principalities ~ princely ranks, dignities, or jurisdictions; princely territories or countries

principality ~ princely rank, dignity, or jurisdiction; princely territory or country

principles ~ basics, fundamentals

printed ~ inscribed

prised ~ prized (Brit): priced, valued, appraised

prisoner ~ *Gk* bound, in chains

privily ~ *Arc* privately, secretly

privy to ~ *Arc* privately informed about

privy ~ *Arc* private

proceedeth ~ proceeds ~ 11

proclaimeth ~ proclaims ~ 1

procureth ~ procures: gets (by effort); obtains

profane ~ make common or unholy: debase, desecrate, defile

profane ~ common, unholy; defiled, debased

profaned ~ made common or unholy: debased, desecrated, defiled

profaneth ~ makes common: debases, desecrates, defiles

profaning ~ making common or unholy: debasing, defiling, desecrating

profited ~ i.e. increased, advanced

profiteth ~ profits ~ 6

progenitors ~ ancestors, forefathers

prognosticators ~ predictors, forecasters, foretellers

prolongeth ~ prolongs ~ 2

promisedst ~ promised ~ 3

proof ~ *Obs* tested or proved strength

proof ~ trial, testing, & approval

proper tongue ~ own language

proper good ~ *Heb* property

proper ~ own; *Arc* fine-looking, handsome

prophesieth ~ prophesies ~ 7

propitiation ~ satisfaction, appeasement, expiation

proselyte ~ convert to Judaism

proselytes ~ converts to Judaism

prospereth ~ prospers ~ 4

prosperously ~ successfully

prosperously effected ~ *Heb* caused to prosper

prostitute ~ sell the services of; *Heb* defile, pollute

protest ~ solemnly affirm, declare

prove ~ test, try; try and approve; approve (after trial); verify, substantiate; give evidence; give evidence for; show

proved ~ tested, tried; tried, and approved; shown, demonstrated

provender ~ fodder, feed; dry animal food

proveth ~ proves ~ 1

providence ~ provision, foresight

provideth ~ provides ~ 2

proving ~ approving

provocation ~ defiance

provoke ~ incite, stir-up

provokedst ~ provoked ~ 1

provoketh ~ provokes ~ 3

prudence ~ practical understanding

psalteries ~ ancient stringed instruments

psaltery ~ ancient stringed instrument

publican ~ tax collector for the Roman Empire

publicans ~ tax collectors for the Roman Empire

publick ~ public ~ 1

publickly ~ publicly ~ 2

publish ~ proclaim, announce

published ~ proclaimed, announced

publisheth ~ publishes ~ 4

puffeth ~ puffs: sniffs, pants, blows

pulpit ~ raised platform

pulse ~ edible seeds of peas, beans, lentils, and similar plants having pods

purchase to ~ i.e. obtain for

purely ~ thoroughly, completely

purged ~ cleansed, purified

purgeth it ~ rids it of impurities, foreign matter, or undesirable elements

purgeth ~ purges ~ 1

purifieth ~ purifies ~ 2

purloining ~ stealing

purple ~ purple (robe)

purposed ~ decided, intended; planned

purposeth ~ purposes ~ 1

purse ~ money bag or money pouch; *Gk* money-belt

purses ~ small bags or pouches for carrying money; *Gk* hollow belts for money-hiding

pursueth ~ pursues ~ 8

purtenance ~ *Arc* the viscera (internal organs) of an animal

put off ~ *Gk* untie

put in trust ~ entrusted

put to ~ put forth, use, exert

put you in remembrance ~ remind you

put her away ~ i.e. divorce her

put away ~ i.e. divorced

putrifying ~ becoming putrid (foul-smelling): rotting, decaying, decomposing (*Heb* fresh, new)

puttest ~ put ~ 7

putteth ~ puts ~ 30

putting you in remembrance ~ *Gk* remind(ing) you

putting you in mind ~ reminding you

pygarg ~ an antelope (or gazelle) with a white rump

quarrel ~ cause for dispute or conflict; angry, resentful grudge or disagreement

quarries ~ kjv margin=graven images

quarter ~ region, district, place

quarters ~ regions, districts, places

quaternions ~ set of four: *Gk* a guard consisting of four soldiers (for among the Romans this was the usual number of the guard to which the custody of captives and prisoners was entrusted; two soldiers were confined with the prisoner and two kept guard outside). Four quaternions of soldiers would be used to guard one all night, one for each of the four night watches.

quench ~ extinguish, put out

quenched ~ extinguished, put out

question ye ~ _Gk_ are ye discussing or disputing

quick ~ rapid; _Arc_ living, alive

quicken ~ revive, enliven, animate; make alive

quickened ~ revived, enlivened; made alive

quickeneth ~ quickens: revives, enlivens; makes alive

quickening ~ life-giving; reviving, enlivening

quieteth ~ quiets ~ 1

quit you ~ _Arc_ conduct yourselves: i.e. act

quit ~ free (from obligation); _Arc_ conduct (oneself)

quite ~ completely, totally

raca ~ empty-head, senseless

rageth ~ rages ~ 1

rail ~ speak bitterly or reproachfully (against, at, or on)

railed on ~ spoke bitterly or reproachfully against

railed ~ spoke bitterly or reproachfully (against)

railer ~ one characterized by bitter, reproachful, abusive speech: reviler

railing ~ bitter, reproachful, abusive speech

railings ~ bitter, reproachful, abusive speeches

raiment ~ _Arc_ clothing, attire, apparel, dress: i.e. covering

raiseth ~ raises ~ 8

raising up ~ stirring up, inciting

rampart ~ bank of earth raised around a fort as a bulwark or defense

ranges ~ i.e. cooking furnaces, stoves

ranges ~ rows, ranks (of soldiers)

ranging ~ roaming, wandering

rank ~ full-grown, robust, ripe, healthy

rase ~ raze: demolish (Brit sp)

rash ~ reckless, too hasty

rattleth ~ rattles ~ 1

ravening ~ greedily searching for prey; plundering, tearing

ravenous ~ greedily or wildly hungry; voracious or famished

ravin ~ greedily devour (alt sp of raven)

ravin ~ torn remnants (alt sp of raven)

ravished ~ seized, carried away by force; raped; enraptured; transported with joy, delight

reacheth ~ reaches ~ 14

readest ~ read ~ 2

readeth ~ reads ~ 4

ready ~ willing

reapest ~ reap ~ 2

reapeth ~ reaps ~ 4

rear up ~ raise, build, erect

rear ~ raise, build, erect

reared ~ raised, i.e. set

reason ~ i.e. reasonable; _Gk_ pleasing, agreeable

reason ye ~ _Gk_ are ye reasoning

rebellest ~ rebel ~ 2

rebuketh ~ rebukes ~ 4

receipt of custom ~ place where tribute, tax, or toll was collected

receivedst ~ received ~ 1

receiveth ~ receives ~ 37

reckon ~ consider, count

reckoned ~ counted, calculated, credited
reckoneth ~ reckons: settles accounts
reckoning ~ accounting
recompence ~ repayment, reward, compensation
recompences ~ repayments, rewards, compensations
recompense ~ repay, reward, compensate
recompensed ~ repaid, rewarded, compensated
recompensest ~ recompense: repay, reward, compensate
recompensing ~ repaying, rewarding, compensating
record ~ witness
recount ~ call to mind, recall; count again
redeemed ~ bought back
redeemedst ~ redeemed ~ 1
redeemeth ~ redeems ~ 2
redound ~ *Arc* overflow; surge up
reformation ~ re-forming; restoring; making straight
refrain ~ *Arc* restrain, curb
refrained ~ restrained
refraineth ~ refrains ~ 1
refresheth ~ refreshes ~ 1
refuge ~ place of safety or protection; shelter from danger
refuse ~ worthless, useless, rejected
refusedst ~ refused ~ 1
refuseth ~ refuses ~ 9
regard **not** ~ do not turn aside to
regard ~ consider, hold in affection or respect; *Arc* show concern for
regarded **them** **not** ~ ignored them
regarded ~ valued; cared for; looked upon
regardest ~ regard ~ 4

regardeth ~ regards: considers; is concerned for; attentively observes; *Arc* shows concern for
regarding ~ considering
regeneration ~ new birth
rehearse ~ recite, repeat, relate, narrate
rehearsed ~ recited, repeated, related, narrated
reignest ~ reign ~ 1
reigneth ~ reigns ~ 13
reins ~ *Arc* kidneys or kidney region; loins: considered as the source of emotions, feelings, or affections
rejecteth ~ rejects ~ 1
rejoicest ~ rejoice ~ 1
rejoiceth ~ rejoices ~ 18
release **to** ~ holiday for
relieveth ~ relieves ~ 1
remainest ~ remain ~ 2
remaineth ~ remains ~ 37
rememberest ~ remember ~ 2
remembereth ~ remembers ~ 5
remembrance ~ memory
remission ~ forgiveness, pardon
remit ~ forgive, pardon
remitted ~ forgiven, pardoned
remnant ~ remainder, rest
removeth ~ removes ~ 5
rend ~ tear, pull apart, split, or rip up with violence
render ~ repay, return, give, present; pay off, repay; give back, return
rendered ~ paid back, repaid; gave back
renderest ~ render: pay back, repay, give
rendereth ~ renders: gives
rending ~ tearing, ripping
renewest ~ renew ~ 2

renown ~ great fame or reputation; celebrity

rent ~ tore (tore, torn, tare), pulled apart, split, or ripped up violence

rentest ~ rent: tear, rip

repayeth ~ repays ~ 1

repeateth ~ repeats ~ 1

repent ~ change your mind (about sin, self, & the Savior)

repentance ~ a change of mind (toward sin, self, & the Savior)

repented them ~ i.e. sorrowed

repented ~ grieved, sorrowed; dissatisfied

repentest ~ repent ~ 1

repenteth ~ repents: sorrows, grieves, saddens; dissatisfies

replenish ~ *Arc* fill; populate; fill or supply with people

repliest ~ reply ~ 1

reproach ~ shame, scorn, disgrace; *Obs* object of blame or scorn

reproached ~ scorned, reviled

reproachest ~ reproach ~ 1

reproacheth ~ reproaches: finds fault with, rebukes

reprobate ~ rejected, condemned, unapproved (after failing a test)

reprobates ~ ones rejected, condemned, unapproved (after failing the test)

reprove ~ rebuke, censure; *Obs* refute, disprove; *Obs* convince, convict

reproved ~ disapproved, censured

reproveth ~ reproves ~ 4

reputation ~ *Gk* honor

reputed ~ considered

requirest ~ require ~ 1

requireth ~ requires ~ 2

requite ~ pay back, reward; avenge, retaliate

requited ~ paid back, repaid; rewarded; avenged, retaliated

requiting ~ paying back, rewarding; avenging

rereward ~ *Arc* rearward: rear-guard- -military detachment that protects the rear of a main body or force

rescueth ~ rescues ~ 1

resemble ~ compare

reserveth ~ reserves ~ 2

residue of ~ rest of [the]

residue ~ rest, remainder

resisteth ~ resists ~ 4

resort ~ go (for help, comfort, aid, or support); *Gk* assemble, come together

resorted ~ came, went (for help, aid, comfort); customarily or often went; went (on a regular basis)

respect of persons ~ improper favor, partiality, or favoritism

respecteth ~ respects ~ 2

respite ~ delay, postponement; relief

restest ~ rest ~ 1

resteth ~ rests ~ 4

restitution ~ reimbursement, restoration

restoreth ~ restores ~ 2

restrainest ~ restrain ~ 1

retained ~ kept

retaineth ~ retains ~ 3

retire ~ retreat

retired ~ retreated

returneth ~ returns ~ 7

revealeth ~ reveals ~ 6

revelation ~ unveiling

revellings ~ noisy feasts; loud merry- making; or any kind of disorderly or immoral festival

revenger ~ punisher

revengeth ~ revenges ~ 2
reverence ~ respect, honor
revile ~ curse, verbally abuse
reviled ~ used abusive language at (or
against); abused with
contemptuous words; verbally
abused
revilest thou ~ Are you verbally
abusing
revilest ~ revile ~ 1
revilings ~ verbal abuse, name calling
rewardeth ~ rewards ~ 6
ribband ~ cord, twisted-thread; *Arc*
form of ribbon)
rid ~ *Arc* deliver, rescue; free; remove
riddance ~ removal, clearance;
deliverance
rideth ~ rides ~ 7
rie ~ rye (*Heb* spelt--a wheat-like crop
planted and harvested in fall
or spring)
rifled ~ plundered, pillaged,
ransacked
right ~ very, extremely
rightly dividing ~ *Gk* right-cutting:
properly handling
rigour ~ rigor: harshness, severity,
difficulty
ringstraked ~ *Obs* ring-streaked:
having bands of color around
the body
riot ~ *Rare* participate in: wild, loose
living; debauchery;
unrestrained revelry
riot ~ *Rare* wild, loose living;
debauchery; unrestrained
revelry; wild, noisy feast or
revel
rioting ~ *Rare* loose living,
debauchery; unrestrained
revelry
riotous ~ shamelessly immoral,
debauched; profligate;

extremely wasteful;
unrestrained
risest ~ rise ~ 2
riseth ~ rises ~ 14
rising ~ i.e. swelling, abscess, tumor,
boil
road ~ *Obs* raid, invasion (*Heb* a
dash)
roareth ~ roars ~ 3
roast ~ roasted
roasteth ~ roasts ~ 2
robbeth ~ robs ~ 1
roe ~ small, agile, graceful Asiatic
and European deer
roes ~ small, agile, graceful Asiatic
and European deer
roll of a book ~ i.e. scroll
roll ~ i.e. scroll
rolleth ~ rolls ~ 1
room ~ place (at the table); place,
position; *Obs* place
rooms ~ places
round about ~
round about ~ all around; i.e. on
either side of
rouse ~ wake
rovers ~ wanderers, i.e. nomads
ruddy ~ reddish, in a healthy way;
healthy, reddish color
rude ~ unlearned, ignorant: unskilled
in any art
rudiments ~ elements, fundamental
principles
rue ~ shrubby plant with bitter tasting
leaves formerly used in
medicine
rulest ~ rule ~ 2
ruleth ~ rules ~ 14
ruling ~ managing
rumour ~ rumor ~ ~ 10
rumours ~ rumors ~ 2
runnest ~ run ~ 1
runneth ~ runs ~ 11

rush ~ grass-like aquatic plant with hollow stems found on banks of rivers, ponds, and marshes

rushes ~ grass-like aquatic plants with hollow stems found on banks of rivers, ponds, and marshes

rusheth ~ rushes ~ 1

sackbut ~ medieval wind instrument, forerunner of the trom-bone (*Heb* a triangular musical instrument with four strings, similar to a lyre)

sacrificedst ~ sacrificed ~ 1

sacrificeth ~ sacrifices ~ 6

said ~ before mentioned

saint ~ holy one

saints ~ holy ones

saith ~ says ~ 1262

saltness ~ saltiness

salutation ~ greeting

salutations ~ greetings

salute ~ greet or welcome with friendly words or respectful gestures

saluted ~ greeted

saluteth ~ greets

saluteth ~ salutes ~ 5

sanctification ~ setting apart, consecration; holiness, purification

sanctified ~ set apart, made holy; consecrated; purified, separated

sanctifieth ~ makes holy, sets apart

sanctifieth ~ sanctifies ~ 4

sanctify ~ set apart, make holy; consecrate; purify, cleanse

sardine ~ red stone from Sardius: (*Gk* a precious stone: either a carnelian [flesh colored] or a sard [red])

satest ~ sat ~ 2

satiate ~ *Rare* satisfied to the full; gratified completely

satiate ~ *Rare* satisfy to the full; gratify completely

satiated ~ *Rare* satisfied to the full; gratified completely

satisfaction ~ reparation, ransom, bribe

satisfiest ~ satisfy ~ 1

satisfieth ~ satisfies ~ 3

satyr ~ in mythology: a minor woodland deity (companion of Bacchus) depicted as having the pointed ears, legs, and short horns of a goat, the head and body of a man, and a fondness for unrestrained revelry and lechery

save ~ except, but

savest ~ save ~ 3

saveth ~ saves ~ 7

saving ~ excepting, but, *Rare* except

saviour ~ savior ~ 37

saviours ~ saviors ~ 2

savour ~ savor: taste or smell

savourest ~ savor: taste with delight, taste; appreciate

savours ~ savors ~ 1

savoury ~ tasty, flavorful

sawest ~ saw ~ 21

sawn ~ cut

say ~ said

sayest ~ say ~ 40

scaleth ~ scales ~ 1

scall ~ any scaly or scabby skin disease, esp of the scalp

scapegoat ~ object upon which the guilt for others' sins falls

scarce ~ Literary: scarcely; *Arc* scarcely

scarest ~ scare ~ 1

scattereth ~ scatters ~ 10

sceptre ~ scepter ~ 15

schism ~ split or division caused by difference of opinion

schoolmaster ~ *Gk* trusted slave who constantly supervised the life & morals of his master's son until adulthood

science ~ knowledge

scoffers ~ mockers

scorn ~ object of extreme, often indignant, contempt or utter disdain

scorn ~ treat with extreme, often indignant, contempt or utter disdain

scorner ~ one who scorns, derides, or mocks; esp one who scoffs at religion

scorners ~ ones who scorn, deride, or mock; esp ones who scoff at religion

scornest ~ scorn: deride, utterly disdain; mock or scoff at

scorneth ~ scorns: derides, utterly disdains; mocks or scoffs at

scornful ~ full of scorn; derisive; boastful, arrogant

scorning ~ mocking, disdain, scoffing, contempt

scourge ~ whip

scourged ~ whipped

scourgeth ~ scourges: whips, flogs

scourging ~ whipping

scourgings ~ whippings

scrabbled ~ scraped, scratched, or groped about wildly or frantically with the hands.

scribe ~ law-copyist & law-expert

scribes ~ law-copyists; law-experts

scrip ~ *Arc* wallet, small bag, or satchel (*Gk* a leathern sack in which travelers & shepherds carried their provisions; a wallet)

sea ~ i.e. large container for water; the temple's largest laver or water container

sealest ~ seal ~ 1

sealeth ~ seals ~ 3

searchest ~ search ~ 2

searcheth ~ searches ~ 8

seared with a hot iron ~ scorched or burned on the surface; branded, cauterized with a hot iron; made callous or unfeeling; hardened

season ~ time; while; brief time; suitable, proper, fitting, or convenient time; *Gk* little (time)

seasons ~ times

seat ~ thrown-seat

seats ~ *Gk* thrown-seats or chairs of state

sect ~ religious faction or group

secure you ~ protect you; *Gk* free you from anxiety

security of ~ sufficient downpayment or bond from

sedition ~ *Arc* revolt, rebellion

seduce you ~ lead you astray

seducers ~ *Gk* deceivers, impostors

seduceth ~ seduces ~ 1

see to ~ i.e. look upon

seed ~ *Arc* descendants, posterity

seeing then that ~ since

seeing that ~ i.e. since, because; *Gk* since

seeing ~ since, because

seekest ~ seek ~ 9

seeketh ~ seeks ~ 42

seemeth ~ seems ~ 28

seemly ~ fitting, pleasing, proper, becoming, appropriate

seest ~ see ~ 36

seeth ~ sees ~ 54

seethe ~ boil or cook by boiling

seething ~ boiling

selfsame ~ the very same, identical

sellest ~ sell ~ 1

selleth ~ sells ~ 7

selvedge ~ a specially woven edge that keeps fabric from unraveling

senate ~ council of elders, Sanhedrin

senators ~ council of elders (*Heb* elders)

sendest ~ send ~ 6

sendeth ~ sends ~ 15

sentence ~ verdict, judgment, decision

sentest ~ sent ~ 4

separateth ~ separates ~ 5

sepulchre ~ tomb, grave, burial vault (Brit spell of sepulcher)

sepulchres ~ tombs, graves, burial vaults (Brit for sepulchers)

serjeants ~ sergeants, court officers; (*Gk* lictors, public officials who bore the fasces or staff and other insignia of office before a magistrate)

serpent ~ snake

serpents ~ snakes

served ~ treated

servedst ~ served ~ 1

servest ~ serve ~ 2

serveth ~ serves ~ 9

servile ~ slavish; befitting a slave: i.e. laborious

servitor ~ servant, attendant

set at liberty ~ released, set free

set at nought ~ *Gk* treated with contempt, utterly despised; (*Heb* ne-glected, ignored)

set at nought of ~ *Gk* treated with contempt by, utterly despised by

set by ~ i.e. valued

set forth ~ put out; *Gk* set sail, put to sea

set him at nought ~ i.e. treated him as if he were nothing (naught); (*Gk* utterly despised him)

set on ~ attack

set on ~ i.e. serve(d)

set them at one again ~ *Gk* urged them unto peace

set to ~ *Arc* affixed

set upon ~ i.e. attack

set light by ~ treated with contempt; dishonored

set your affection ~ *Gk* focus your mind

set a compass ~ *Arc* traced or inscribed a circle

set ~ put, placed; i.e. went

setter forth ~ proclaimer

settest ~ set ~ 7

setteth thee on ~ incites, urges you on

setteth light by ~ *Heb* dishonors, treats with contempt or shame

setteth ~ sets ~ 22

setting a watch ~ i.e. assigning soldiers to guard

settle ~ *Obs* sitting place, ledge, or raised platform

settlest ~ settle ~ 1

sevenfold ~ seven times

sever out ~ set apart, separate, or make a distinction

sever ~ set apart, separate, divide, or make a distinction

several ~ separate

severally ~ separately, independently

severed ~ separated, or set apart

sewest ~ sew ~ 1

seweth ~ sews ~ 1

shaketh ~ shakes ~ 7

shalt ~ shall ~ 1617

shambles ~ *Rare* place where meat is sold; butcher's stall or shop (Brit)

shamefacedness ~ great modesty, bashfulness, or shyness (*Gk* a sense of shame, modesty, bashfulness)

shameth ~ shames ~ 1

share ~ plow part that cuts the soil: plowshare

sharpeneth ~ sharpens ~ 3

she asses ~ female donkeys, burros

she ~ female

sheaves ~ bundles of harvested grain

shed forth ~ poured out

shed abroad ~ *Gk* poured out

shed ~ poured out

sheddeth ~ sheds ~ 2

sheepcote ~ small shelter or shed for sheep; sheepfold

sheepcotes ~ small shelters or sheds for sheep; sheepfolds

sherd ~ shard--fragment or broken piece, esp of pottery; potsherd

sherds ~ shards--fragments or broken pieces, esp of pottery; potsherds

shew of ~ *Gk* proclaim or declare concerning

shew ~ show; display, declare

shew ~ show: false display, fake performance

shewbread ~ showbread ~ 18

shewed ~ showed: revealed, displayted

shewedst ~ shewed, ~ showed ~ 2

shewest ~ shew, ~ show ~ 5

sheweth ~ shews, ~ shows ~ 20

shewing ~ *Gk* public showing forth

shineth ~ shines ~ 9

shittim ~ an Asiatic acacia with close grained yellowish-brown wood (*Heb* acacia)

Shittim ~ city named for close-grained yellowish-brown wood

shivers ~ fragments, chips, splinters, slivers

shock ~ stacked sheaf

shod ~ shoed: provided with shoes

shoelatchet ~ *Arc* lace or strap that binds a shoe or sandal

shoot forth ~ put out leaves

shooteth ~ shoots ~ 3

shorn ~ cut short the hair of; given a short hair-cut

short space ~ *Gk* little (time)

shouldest ~ should ~ 73

shouteth ~ shouts ~ 1

shroud ~ (*Arc*) cover

shun ~ avoid

shunned ~ hesitated

shut up ~ i.e. imprisoned

shut to ~ *Obs* securely closed or bolted

shutteth ~ shuts ~ 8

sighest ~ sigh ~ 1

sigheth ~ sighs ~ 1

sign ~ authenticating demonstration or miracle

signet ~ seal, esp one used as a signature in marking a document as official; sealing ring

signets ~ seals, esp ones used as a signature in marking a document as official; sealing rings

signified ~ made known by signs or symbols

signifieth ~ signifies ~ 1

signs ~ hand-signals

signs ~ authenticating miracles

silverlings ~ *Arc* shekels (half-ounce Hebrew silver coins)

silversmith ~ artisan who makes or repairs silver objects, esp by shaping the metal while it is hot and soft

similitude ~ likeness, form

similitudes ~ *Obs* allegories, parables, similes

simple ~ someone innocent, easily misled, or ignorant (*Heb* naive, open-minded, foolish)

simplicity ~ generosity; genuineness

sincere ~ without deceit, pretense, or hypocrisy; genuine; *Gk* found pure when unfolded and examined by the sun's light; *Gk* unadulterated, pure

singeth ~ sings ~ 1

single ~ *Gk* sound, healthy

singleness ~ simplicity, sincerity, mental honesty

singular ~ extraordinary

sinnest ~ sin ~ 1

sinneth ~ sins ~ 22

Sion ~ Zion ~ 9

sith ~ *Arc* since

sittest ~ sit ~ 7

sitteth ~ sits ~ 42

situate ~ *Arc* situated: placed, located

situation ~ location, position

sixscore ~ one hundred twenty (a score=20)

skippedst ~ skipped ~ 1

skirt ~ i.e. bottom part

slack ~ delay, hesitate, be slow; relax, delay, slow

slack ~ slow; negligent; idle; hesitant; sluggish, loose

slackness ~ slowness, sluggishness; delay

slain ~ kill(ed) or destroyed in a violent way; kill (i.e. animals for food)

slanderest ~ slander ~ 1

slandereth ~ slanders ~ 1

slayeth ~ slays: kills or destroys in a violent way

slaying ~ killing or destroying in a violent way

sleep ~ i.e. are dead

sleepest ~ sleep ~ 4

sleepeth ~ sleeps ~ 7

sleight ~ cunning or craft used in deception

slept ~ i.e. died

slew ~ kill(ed) or destroy(ed) in a violent way

slewest ~ slew, ~ killed ~ 1

slideth ~ slides ~ 1

slime ~ pitch, bitumen, asphalt

slimepits ~ pits or holes yielding asphalt or bitumen

slippeth ~ slips ~ 3

slips ~ stems, roots, twigs, etc. cut or broken off a plant and used for planting or grafting; cuttings, scions

slothful ~ sluggish, slow, lazy, inactive

slothfulness ~ sluggishness, laziness, inactivity

slow bellies ~ i.e. lazy gluttons

sluggard ~ habitually lazy or idle person

sluices ~ artificial channels or passages for water, having a gate or valve at their heads to regulate the flow

slumbereth ~ slumbers: sleeps

smart ~ suffer pain

smelleth ~ smells ~ 1

smite out ~ knock out

smite ~ *Rare* strike or hit hard; attack; destroy; kill

smitest ~ smite: hit or strike hard

smiteth through ~ *Rare* hits or strikes hard; attacks; destroys; kills

smiteth ~ smites: *Rare* hits or strikes hard; attacks; destroys; kills

smith ~ person who makes or repairs metal objects, esp by shaping metal while it is hot & soft; metalworker

smiting ~ *Rare* striking or hitting hard; attacking; destroying; killing

smitten ~ *Rare* struck or hit hard; attacked; destroyed; killed

smootheth ~ smoothes ~ 1

smote ~ *Rare* struck or hit hard; destroyed; killed

smotest ~ smote: *Rare* struck, hit hard

snare ~ noose-like trap for catching small animals

snared ~ caught in a noose-like trap used for small animals

snares ~ noose-like traps for small animals

snuffed ~ sniffed

snuffeth ~ snuffs: sniffs

so much the more ~ i.e. even more

sobriety ~ *Gk* self-control; a sound mind

sod ~ boiled

sodden ~ boiled

sodoma ~ i.e. Sodom

sodomite ~ a person who practices sodomy--any sexual intercourse held to be abnormal, esp anal intercourse between two male persons or bestiality (*Heb* a male temple prostitute)

sodomites ~ persons who practice sodomy--any sexual intercourse held to be abnormal, esp anal intercourse between two male persons or

bestiality (*Heb* male temple prostitutes)

soever ~ i.e. whatever

sojourn ~ stay, dwell, or live temporarily

sojourned ~ stayed, dwelt, or lived temporarily

sojourner ~ visitor, temporary resident

sojourneth ~ sojourns: stays, dwells, or lives temporarily

sojourning ~ temporarily stay or staying temporarily

solace ~ comfort, soothe, console, relieve

solemnity ~ solemn ceremony, ritual

solitary ~ lonely, isolated, alone

some time ~ *Arc* formerly

sometime ~ *Arc* formerly

sometimes ~ *Arc* formerly; *Gk* once, formerly

somewhat ~ i.e. something, anything

somewhat ~ to some degree or extent; a little

soothsayer ~ one who professes to foretell the future

soothsayers ~ ones who profess to foretell the future

soothsaying ~ making predictions

sop ~ piece of bread dipped in liquid before eating

sorcerers ~ wizards

sorceries ~ magic arts, witchcraft; black magic; witchery

sore ~ *Heb* plague spot, plague, disease, stroke

sore ~ *Arc* exceedingly great, severe; greatly, extremely, exceedingly, greatly

sorely ~ *Arc* severely, greatly

sorer ~ *Arc* greater, worse

sorroweth ~ sorrows ~ 1

sottish ~ like a sot (drunkard): stupid
   or foolish as from too much
   drinking
sound ~ healthy
sounded ~ probed the depths of, i.e.
   thoroughly questioned
sounded ~ measured water depth
soundeth ~ sounds ~ 1
sow ~ female pig
sowedst ~ sowed ~ 1
sowest ~ sow ~ 3
soweth ~ sows ~ 15
space ~ time
spake ~ spoke ~ 598
spakest ~ spake, ~ spoke ~ 10
span ~ distance from extended pinky
   to thumb; i.e. about nine
   inches
spareth ~ spares ~ 4
sparingly ~ in a stingy, sparing
   manner
speakest ~ speak ~ 17
speaketh ~ speaks ~ 74
specially ~ *Obs* especially
speed ~ success, fortune
spendest ~ spend ~ 1
spendeth ~ spends ~ 3
spent ~ used up
spied ~ saw, observed; seen
spikenard ~ very fragrant ointment or
   oil derived from the head or
   spike of the nard plant; liquid
   or pure nard
spitefully entreated ~ shamefully or
   maliciously *Arc* treated
spitefully ~ shamefully
spittle ~ spit, saliva
spoil ~ plundering, looting; *Heb*
   devastation, ruin
spoil ~ goods or territory taken by
   force in war; plunder;
   devastation, ruin

spoil ~ take goods by force in war,
   plunder, loot;
spoiled ~ ruined; *Arc* robbed,
   pillaged, plundered, looted
spoilers ~ plunderers, looters,
   pillagers; robbers
spoilest ~ spoil ~ 1
spoileth ~ spoils: takes goods by force
   in war, plunders, loots
spoiling ~ taking goods by force in
   war, plundering, looting
spoils ~ goods taken in battle, plunder
sporting themselves with ~ reveling
   or delighting in
sporting ~ (amorously) playing or
   frolicking,
spreadest ~ spread ~ 1
spreadeth ~ spreads ~ 14
spreading ~ scattering, dispersing
springeth ~ springs ~ 4
springs ~ sources, origins, motives
sprinkleth ~ sprinkles ~ 2
spue ~ spew: vomit
spued ~ spewed ~ 1
spy out ~ i.e. view
stablish ~ *Arc* establish: make stable,
   firm; strengthen, settle,
   confirm, stabilize; fulfill;
   cause to happen
stablished ~ *Arc* established: settled
stablisheth ~ stablishes: *Arc*
   establishes
staggereth ~ staggers ~ 1
stanched ~ stopped (mod sp
   staunched)
stand to it ~ i.e. stands firm
standard ~ flag or banner
standards ~ flags or banners
standest ~ stand ~ 6
standeth ~ stands ~ 30
stank ~ stunk, i.e. were very offensive
state ~ condition

stature ~ height
staves ~ staffs: poles (alt pl)
stay ~ support; wait, i.e. delay; stop,
  i.e. standstill
stay ~ restrain, hold back, remain,
  refrain; hinder ; wait, i.e.
  delay; stop, i.e. standstill;
  (*Heb* make to lie down); rely;
  support, sustain, supply
stayed ~ fixed
stayed ~ halted, stopped; held back;
  propped; restrained, detained;
  remained; remained, relied,
  leaned; waited
stayeth ~ stays: stops, restrains
stays ~ supports
stead ~ place
steads ~ places
stealeth ~ steals ~ 3
stedfast ~ firmly fixed; steadfastly:
  firmly, strongly
stedfastly ~ unwaveringly, constantly
stedfastness ~ firmness of belief
steemeth ~ considers, judges
steppeth ~ steps ~ 1
steward ~ estate or household
  manager
stewards ~ managers of a large estate
sticketh ~ sticks ~ 1
still ~ silent, quiet; silence
stilled ~ quieted
stillest ~still: quiet, calm
stilleth ~ stills: quiets
stingeth ~ stings ~ 1
stinketh ~ stinks ~ 2
stir ~ disturbance; commotion,
  agitation
stirreth ~ stirs ~ 8
stirs ~ shakings, agitations; *Heb*
  noises
stock ~ *Arc* wooden block or log
stock ~ lineage, family

stocks ~ blocks of wood, logs
stomacher ~ richly ornamented,
  triangular piece of cloth
  formerly worn, esp by women
  as a covering for the chest or
  abdomen
stones ~ *Arc* testicles
stonest ~ stone ~ 2
stoodest ~ stood ~ 3
stoopeth ~ stoops ~ 1
stopped ~ closed up; muzzled; shut;
  blocked
stoppeth ~ stops ~ 4
store to ~ supply or reserve for
store ~ storage, reserve; abundance;
  supply
stories ~ (heavenly) *Heb* steps, stairs,
  levels
stout ~ forceful, powerful
straightway ~ immediately
strait ~ *Arc* narrow or confining;
  narrow place--i.e. difficulty or
  difficult
straiten them ~ *Arc* restrict them
  closely, hem them in
straitened ~ *Arc* closely restricted,
  hemmed in
straiteneth ~ *Arc* narrows, restricts
straiteneth ~ straitens ~ 1
straitest ~ *Arc* strictest
straitly ~ *Arc* strictly, urgently
straitness ~ *Arc* distress, confinement
straits ~ *Arc* narrows or narrow
  places--i.e. difficulties
strake sail ~ lowered the sail
strakes ~ *Arc* streaks; strips; stripes
strange ~ foreign, alien
strawed ~ *Arc* strewed--scattered
strengthenedst ~ strengthened ~ 1
strengtheneth ~ strengthens ~ 7
stretchedst ~ stretched ~ 1
stretchest ~ stretch ~ 1

stretcheth ~ stretches ~ 7
stricken in ~ struck by : i.e. along in
strife ~ conflict: quarrel, dispute,
     struggle; *Gk* contradiction,
     opposition
strifes of words ~ word-battles
strifes ~ fights
striker ~ striking or punching addict
striketh ~ strikes ~ 3
stripes ~ whip-strokes, long skin-
     welts; blood-trickling wounds;
     Arc strokes with a whip; long
     welts on the skin; lashes of a
     whip; welts
stripling ~ one as thin as a strip:
     youth, young person
stript ~ stripped ~ 1
strive ~ fight, struggle; argue, debate;
     compete
strived ~ struggled, agonized, fought
striveth ~ strives ~ 2
striving ~ struggling, battles
strove ~ contended, struggled; fought;
     Obs vied
strowed ~ *Arc* strewed--scattered
stubble ~ short stumps of grain left
     standing
studieth ~ studies: ponders; tries hard
study ~ try hard; *Gk* be diligent
stuff ~ household or personal
     possessions; household goods,
     belongings
stumbleth ~ stumbles ~ 4
subduedst ~ subdued ~ 1
subdueth ~ subdues ~ 3
subject unto ~ submissive to, under
     the authority of
subject to like passions ~ *Gk* of
     similar feelings
subject ~ submissive, obedient; being
     subjected, submitting

subjection ~ *Obs* obedience,
     submission; *Gk* slavery: stern,
     rigid discipline
submit ~ under-rank; subordinate
suborned ~.bribed
substance ~ wealth, property,
     possessions
subtil ~ subtle: crafty, sly
subtilly ~ *Rare* spell of subtilely:
     craftily, slyly
subtilty ~ craftiness, deceit, guile,
     trickery; deception; (*Rare*
     spell)
suburbs ~ areas located just outside
     of a city
subvert ~ overturn, corrupt
subverted ~ turned inside out,
     corrupted
succeedest ~ succeed ~ 2
succour ~ succor: help, aid, rescue in
     time of need
succoured ~ succored: helped, aided,
     rescued in time of need
succourer ~ succorer: helper (in time
     of need)
such like ~ suchlike: similar, in like
     manner; of such a kind
suckling ~ unweaned or nursing child
sucklings ~ unweaned or nursing
     children
suffer ~ endure, permit, allow,
     tolerate, put up with; let;
     experience
suffer ~ permit, allow
suffered ~ permitted, tolerated;
     experienced, endured;
     allowed; let
sufferest ~ suffer: tolerate, permit,
     allow
suffereth long ~ endures for a long
     time

suffereth ~ suffers: experiences; endures; permits

suffice ~ *Arc* satisfy, be enough for

sufficed them not ~ i.e. were not enough

sufficed ~ satisfied

sufficeth ~ suffices: *Arc* satisfies

sufficient unto ~ enough for

sum ~ total, count; i.e. summary

sunder ~ pieces, parts

sundered ~ separated, split apart

sundry ~ various, diverse

sup up ~ eat the evening meal; have supper; gobble up

sup ~ eat the evening meal; have supper

superfluity ~ overflowing, superabundance

superfluous ~ unnecessary, not needed

superscription ~ inscription or engraving on top or outer surface; surface inscription; *Gk* inscription, title

. **supped** ~ eaten the evening meal

supplant ~ take the place of through force or plotting

supplanted ~ uprooted, replaced, esp through treachery

supple ~ soften

suppliants ~ petitioners

supplication ~ humble request, prayer, petition, pea

supplications ~ humble requests, petitions, or pleas

supplieth ~ supplies ~ 2

sure ~ certain, secure, firm

surely ~ certainly

surety ~ certainty; one responsible for another's debts; legally responsible; contract

surfeiting ~ overindulgence, gluttony, excess

surmisings ~ conjectures, guesses

surname ~ other name; nickname; i.e. also named; *Obs* second or other name

sustenance ~ nourishment, food

swaddled ~ swathed, bound, or wrapped with strips of cloth

swaddling clothes ~ long, narrow bands of cloth wrapped around a newborn in former times

swaddlingband ~ swathing, wrapping cloth or band

swalloweth ~ swallows ~ 2

swarest ~ sware, ~ swore ~ 5

sweareth ~ swears ~ 11

swelling ~ arrogant, prideful

swellings ~ arrogance, pride

swimmest ~ swim ~ 1

swimmeth ~ swims ~ 1

swine ~ pigs

sworn ~ promised with an oath to

sycamine ~ mulberry tree

sycomore ~ sycamore ~ 7

Syriack ~ Aramaic

Syrian ~ Aramaic

tabering ~ beating of a drum

tabernacle ~ *Arc* temporary shelter, tent

tabernacles ~ *Arc* temporary shelters, tents

tables ~ thin, flat tablets used for inscriptions

tables ~ tablets; small flat things to wear as an ornament

tabret ~ small drum

tabrets ~ small drums

taches ~ *Arc* devices for fastening two parts together, fasteners: clasps, buckles, hooks

take **account** ~ settle accounts

take **care for** ~ worry, concern himself about

take **heed** ~ pay close attention to; listen carefully; beware

take **no thought** ~ *Gk* do not worry or be anxious; *Gk* stop worrying

take **ye thought** ~ *Gk* worry or be anxious; do ye worry

taken our leave one of ~ said good-by to one

takest ~ take ~ 9

taketh ~ takes: grasps, captures

taking my leave of ~ saying farewell to

taking thought ~ *Gk* worrying

tale ~ *Arc* tally, count, enumeration

talebearer ~ gossip, slanderer

talents ~ talent=large unit of weight or money; *Gk* In Israel, a talent of silver weighed about 100 pounds (45 kg); and a talent of gold weighed about 200 pounds (91 kg).

talkest ~ talk ~ 3

talketh ~ talks ~ 2

tare ~ tore

tares ~ vetch, darnel, or weeds in general

target ~ small shield, esp a round one; buckler

targets ~ small shields, esp a round ones; bucklers

tarried ~ remained, stayed, waited; delayed (his arrival)

tarriest ~ tarry: wait

tarrieth ~ tarries ~ 2

tarry ~ remain temporarily, remain for a time; remain, wait, delay, hesitate, linger

tarry abroad ~ i.e. remain outdoors, or outside

tarrying ~ delay

tasteth ~ tastes ~ 1

tattlers ~ gossips

taught ~ i.e. instructed

taxing ~ *Gk* registration, census (for taxing purposes)

teachest ~ teach ~ 8

teacheth ~ teaches ~ 16

teareth ~ tears ~ 6

teats ~ nipples

tedious ~ long-winded, boring

teil ~ linden or lime tree

tell ~ count, enumerate, reckon

tellest ~ tell ~ 1

telleth ~ tells: *Arc* counts

temper ~ *Arc* mix (in proper proportions)

temperance ~ self-control; self-restraint

temperate ~ self-controlled; self-restrained

tempered ~ *Arc* mixed (in proper proportions)

tempest ~ violent storm with strong winds

tempestuous ~ stormy, violent

temporal ~ temporary

tempt ~ test or try

temptation ~ testing, trial

temptations ~ testings or trials of any kind

tempted ~ tested, put to the test, tried

tempted of ~ tested, tried by

tempteth ~ tempts ~ 1

tempting ~ testing

tendeth ~ tends ~ 5

tenons ~ projections on the end or side of wood that fit into corresponding holes or cavities in another place

tenor ~ general tendency or meaning

teraphim ~ small images or other things representing household gods, used among ancient Semitic peoples: idols

terrestrial ~ earthly, worldly

terrible ~ fear-producing, fearful, awe-inspiring, terror-inspiring, terror-causing, terror-producing, terrifying

terrifiest ~ terrify ~ 1

testament ~ covenant (esp between God and man); *Rare* will

testator ~ person who has drawn up a will

testifiedst ~ testified ~ 2

testifieth ~ testifies ~ 5

tetrarch ~ ruler of part (one fourth) of a Roman province

thank ~ thanks, reward

thankworthy ~ worthy of thanks, commendable

that ~ i.e. what; i.e. also; *Gk* this that; *Gk* what or that

that thine is ~ i.e. what is thine

the deep ~ Poetic: the sea or the ocean

the dropsy ~ *Obs* edema: fluid over-accumulation

the even ~ *Arc* the evening

the transgression of the law ~ lawlessness

the ministry ~ *Gk* service

the more ~ i.e. even more; to a greater degree

the more carefully ~ *Gk* speedily, hastily, diligently

the more silence ~ i.e. even more silent

the multitude ~ a host, great number

the preeminence ~ the surpassing excellence; *Gk* first place

thee ~ you (singular) ~ 3826-

thee-ward ~toward you (singular) ~ 1-

theeward ~ toward you (singular)

thence ~ *Arc* there; (from) that place or time

thenceforth ~ from that time onward; after that; thereafter

thenceforth ~ therefore

thereabout ~ about this

thereat ~ there; at that place or time

thereby ~ by this or by it

therefore ~ therefore; for this reason; for which cause; *Arc* why?

therefrom ~ from it; from them

therein ~ in there, in it, in them

thereinto ~ into it

thereof ~ of it

thereon ~ on it; on that

thereout ~ out of it

thereto ~ to it

thereunto ~ unto it

thereupon ~ upon it

therewith ~ with it, with which, with them

thicket ~ thick growth of shrubs

thine ~ your (singular) ~ 937 ~ yours (singular) ~ 21-

thinkest ~ think ~ 9

thinketh ~ thinks ~ 6

thirsteth ~ thirsts ~ 4

thirtyfold ~ thirty times (as much)

this wise ~ this way

thither ~ there; to or toward that place

thitherward ~ *Rare* toward that place; there

thongs ~ leather straps

thou ~ you (singular) ~ 5473-

thought ~ thought [it]

thought scorn ~ rejected as disgraceful; utterly disdained

thoughtest ~ thought ~ 1

thoughts ~ *Gk* doubts, hesitations

threescore ~ sixty (a score=20)

thresheth ~ threshes ~ 1

threwest ~ threw ~ 1

thrice ~ three times

throng ~ crowd or press upon in large numbers

thronged ~ pressed against

thronging ~ pressing against

throughly ~ *Arc* completely

throughly furnished ~ completely equipped

throughly purge ~ completely cleanse

thrust in ~ *Gk* drive, propel

thrusteth ~ thrusts ~ 1

thundereth ~ thunders ~ 3

thus.~ in this manner

thy ~ your (singular) ~ 4603-

thyine ~ the citrus, an odoriferous North African tree used as incense, prized by the ancient Greeks and Romans on account of the beauty of its wood for various ornamental purposes

thyself ~ yourself ~ 215-

tidings ~ news

till ~ until

till ~ cultivate

tillage ~ cultivating of land to raise crops, as by plowing, fertilizing etc.; land that is cultivated

tillest ~ till: cultivate

tilleth ~ tills ~ 2

timbrel ~ ancient type of tambourine or drum

timbrels ~ ancient type of tambourines or drums

time ~ i.e. delay

times ~ i.e. periods of time

Ttimotheus ~ Timothy ~ 19

tire ~ *Arc* attire: head-dress, turban

tired her head ~ attired her head, i.e. arranged her hair

tires ~ *Arc* attires: head-dresses

tithes ~ tenth portions or parts

title ~ *Obs* inscription on a sign or placard

tittle ~ small pen-stroke (*Gk* "little horn"--used by grammarians of the accents and diacritical points. Jesus used it of the little lines or projections, by which the Hebrew letters in other respects similar differ from one another; the meaning is, "not even the minutest part of the law shall perish".)

to ~ i.e. as his; i.e. to be his; i.e. as; i.e. [something] to

to and fro ~ back and forth

to edification ~ *Gk* towards building up

to God-ward ~ *Arc* toward God

to morrow ~ tomorrow

to pledge ~ i.e. as a down-payment or collateral

to the intent ~ i.e. so that; *Gk* so that, in order that

to the intent that ~ *Gk* so that, in order that

to the mercy seatward ~ toward the mercy seat

to the spoil ~ i.e. as goods or territory taken by force in war

to their minister ~ for or as their assistant, attendant

to us-ward ~ *Arc* toward us

to wit ~ *Arc* that is to say, namely; for example

to you-ward ~ *Arc* toward you (plural)

token ~ sign or symbol (of genuineness, assurance, or authority)

tokens ~ signs or symbols (of genuineness, assurance, or authority)

told ~ counted, enumerated, reckoned

took ~ mistook

took ~ boarded a; *Gk* stepped or went into a

took his leave of ~ said good-by to

took knowledge of ~ recognized

took shipping ~ *Gk* got into boats

took to wife ~ i.e. married

tookest ~ took ~ 2

torment ~ torture

tormented ~ tortured

tormentors ~ *Gk* torturers

torments ~ tortures

tottering ~ unstable, unsteady

toucheth ~ touches ~ 40

touching ~ concerning, with regard to

tow ~ the coarse and broken fibers of flax, hemp, etc. prepared for spinning

toward ~ favorable towards

traffick ~ traffic: trade (*Arc* sp)

traffickers ~ traffickers: traders

train ~ caravan

transfigured ~ transformed, metamorphosized

transgress ~ overstep, break

transgressest ~ transgress ~ 1

transgresseth the law ~ practices lawlessness

transgresseth ~ transgresses ~ 4

transgressor ~ lawbreaker

translate ~ transfer or transport: move from place or condition to another

translated ~ transferred or transported: moved from one place or condition to another

translation ~ transfer or transport: move from one place or condition to another

travail ~ toil, work very hard; painfully labor; agonize; sudden, sharp, and brief pains--physical or emotional; spasms of distress; labor pains, pains of childbirth; agony, intense pain

travail with child ~ experience labor-pains

travailed ~ toiled, worked very hard: went into labor, began to give birth

travailest ~ travail: labors in birth (*Gk* feels childbirth's labor/ pain)

travaileth ~ travails ~ 7

travaileth ~ toils, works very hard: experiences labor pains

travailing ~ birth-giving, laboring (with the birth process)

travelled ~ traveled

traveller ~ traveler

travelleth ~ travels ~ 2

travelling ~ traveling

tread ~ walk, trample

treadeth ~ treads: tramples, threshes

treasurest ~ treasure ~ 1

treatise ~ *Obs* narrative

tree ~ i.e. cross

trembleth ~ trembles ~ 4

trespass ~ do wrong; cross the line, sin; go beyond the limits of justice or morality

tresspass ~ going beyond the limits of justice or morality

trial ~ *Obs* experience

tribulation ~ great misery or distress; affliction; oppression, suffering

tribulations ~ great miseries or distresses; afflictions, sufferings

tributaries ~ forced laborers; subject nations

tributary ~ under the control of another nation

tribute ~ forced service or required payment; tax levied on a conquered nation; subject-nation tax; i.e. "contribution"

tricketh ~ trickles ~ 1

triest ~ try ~ 3

trieth ~ tries ~ 5

trimmest ~ trim ~ 1

trodden ~ trampled

trode ~ trampled

troop ~ group or body of soldiers

troubledst ~ troubled ~ 1

troublest ~ trouble ~ 1

troubleth ~ troubles ~ 10

trow ~ *Arc* think, suppose, believe

trump ~ trumpet

trustedst ~ trusted ~ 3

trustest ~ trust ~ 6

trusteth ~ trusts ~ 3

tumult ~ uproar, noisy commotion; loud noise, din; noisy confusion

tumults ~ uproars, noisy commotions

turn ~ return

turnest ~ turn ~ 3

turneth ~ turns ~ 33

turtle ~ *Arc* turtledove

turtles ~ *Arc* for turtledoves

tutors ~ legal guardians (*Gk* ones who have the care & tutelage of children whether father be dead or alive)

twain ~ two (*Arc* variant)

twined ~ intertwined, woven, twisted, interlaced

unawares ~ unintentionally, without knowing or being aware; unexpectedly, suddenly, by surprise

unblameable and unreproveable ~ *Gk* without blemish & blame

uncomely ~ unattractive; unbecoming; improper (*Gk* deformed; unseemly, indecent)

uncovereth ~ uncovers ~ 3

unction ~ anointing

under colour ~ i.e. pretending

undersetters ~ supports, bases (*Obs*)

understandest ~ understand ~ 4

understandeth ~ understands ~ 11

undressed ~ unattended, not cultivated

unfeigned ~ genuine, real; sincere

ungirded ~ unbound, unloaded

unicorn ~ *Obs* one-horned rhinoceros: used in the Middle English O.T. to render the Latin Vulgate unicornis or rhinoceros and retained in later versions (*Heb* probably the great aurochs or wild bulls which are now extinct. The exact meaning is not known.)

unicorns ~ *Obs* one-horned rhinoceroses: used in the Middle English O.T. to render the Latin Vulgate unicornis or rhinoceros and retained in later versions (*Heb* probably the great aurochs or wild bulls which are now extinct. The exact meaning is not known.)

unlade ~ unload, unburden (Rare)

unquenchable ~ that can not be put out or extinguished

unruly ~ not subject to rules; unrestrained

unsatiable ~ insatiable: not able to be satisfied

unsearchable ~ incomprehensible

unseemly ~ indecent or improper; indecently or improperly

unshod ~ without shoes; barefooted

unspeakable ~ indescribable, description-defying

untempered ~ *Arc* unmixed (in proper proportions)

untimely birth ~ premature birth, miscarriage

untimely ~ premature: unripe

unto ~ to [in the view of]; *Gk* until

untoward ~ *Arc* stubborn, unruly

unwashen ~ unwashed

unwittingly ~ unknowingly

up ~ i.e. get up; i.e. go up

upbraid ~ rebuke severely or bitterly; censure sharply; scold

upbraided ~ rebuked severely or bitterly; censured sharply; scolded

upbraideth ~ upbraids: rebukes severely or bitterly; censures sharply; scolds

upholdest ~ uphold ~ 1

upholdeth ~ upholds ~ 4

uppermost rooms ~ most prestigious places

urgent ~ insistent

used ~ (mis)treated

used to push ~ i.e. often tried to gore

usest ~ use ~ 1

useth ~ uses ~ 7

usurer ~ one who lends at (excessively high) interest

usurp ~ unjustly take or assume

usury ~ lending at (excessively high) interest; loans at (excessively high) interest; (excessively high) interest

utmost ~ outermost, farthest

utter ~ complete, total; absolute

utter ~ outer, outward, external

utter ~ speak, tell; make known;

utterance ~ words, speech; *Gk* logos: discourse, speech, words

uttereth ~ utters ~ 9

utterly ~ completely, totally

uttermost ~ outermost, farthest, most distant or remote

vagabond ~ wandering, vagrant, shiftless

vagabond ~ wanderer, vagrant, nomad, drifter, tramp

vagabonds ~ wanderers, vagrants, transients, drifters

vail ~ veil: curtain

vain ~ empty, worthless, futile; useless

vain jangling ~ foolish, idle, annoying, angry, or meaningless talk

vainglory ~ extreme self-pride and boastfulness; excessive & ostentatious vanity

vale ~ valley (Poetic)

valiant ~ courageous, brave; strong

valour ~ valor: courage, boldness, bravery

valuest ~ value ~ 1

vanisheth ~ vanishes ~ 2

vanities ~ things vain, futile, idle, or worthless

vanity ~ futility, idleness, or worthlessness; emptiness; something truly vain, futile, idle, or worthless

vapour ~ vapor ~ 5

vapours ~ vapors ~ 3

variableness ~ variation, change

vaunt ~ boast or brag

vaunteth ~ vaunts ~ 1

vehement ~ strong, ardent, vigorous, intense

vehemently ~ strongly, ardently, vigorously, intensely

veil ~ curtain

vein ~ Geology. A regularly shaped and lengthy occurrence of an ore; a lode

vengeance ~ revenge, punishment; avenging justice

venison ~ *Obs* flesh of a game animal used as food

verily ~ *Arc* truly, in very truth

verity ~ truth

vermilion ~ bright red mercuric sulfide used as a pigment: bright red or scarlet color

very chiefest ~ i.e. most important

vessel ~ container; *Obs* body

vestments ~ gowns, robes (esp those used ceremonially)

vestry ~ room for storing or putting on vestments

vesture ~ *Rare* clothing, garment, apparel

vex ~ trouble, disturb; distress, afflict

vexation ~ trouble, distress

vexations ~ troubles, distresses

vexed ~ troubled, disturbed; distressed, afflicted

vial ~ small container for liquids: (*Heb* flask; *Gk* broad, shallow bowl)

vials ~ small containers for liquids; *Gk* shallow bowl(s)

victual ~ food or provisions

victuals ~ articles of food; supplies, sustenance, provisions

vigilant ~ watchful, alert

vile ~ morally base or evil, wicked, depraved, sinful; repulsive disgusting; degrading, base

vilely ~ in a manner morally base or evil, wicked, depraved, sinful; repulsive disgusting; degrading

viler ~ more morally base or evil, wicked, depraved, sinful; repulsive disgusting; degrading

vilest ~ most morally base or evil, wicked, depraved

villany ~ villainy: wicked, detestable, or disgraceful things

vintage ~ grape gathering or time of grape gathering

viol ~ any of an early family of stringed instruments used chiefly in 15th & 16th centuries in sizes from bass viol to treble viol (akin to base fiddle & violin)

viols ~ any of an early family of stringed instruments used chiefly in the 15th & 16th centuries in sizes from bass viol to treble viol (akin to base fiddle & violin)

viper ~ poisonous snake

vipers ~ poisonous snakes

virtue ~ moral excellence: chastity, merit, valor; effective power or force, esp the power to heal or strengthen

visage ~ countenance, face, expression; appearance

visit ~ bring reward, aid, or assistance; inflict punishment, suffering, or judgment (to)

visitation ~ esp, the bringing of punishment, suffering, or judgment, as by God; the

bringing of reward, aid, or
assistance
visited ~
visited ~ inflicted punishment,
suffering, or judgment;
brought reward, aid, or
assistance to·
visited me ~ brought me aid or
comfort
visitest ~visit: bring reward, aid, or
assistance unto
visiteth ~ visits: inflicts punishment,
suffering, or judgment
visiting ~ bringing or inflicting
punishment, suffering, or
judgment upon
vocation ~ calling
void ~ empty; useless, ineffective;
invalid; useless, ineffective
volume ~ scroll, roll
vomiteth ~ vomits ~ 1
vowedst ~ vowed ~ 1
vowest ~ vow ~ 2
voweth ~ vows ~ 1
wail ~ *Gk* beat their breasts for grief
waiteth ~ waits ~ 11
wakeneth ~ wakens ~ 2
waketh ~ wakes ~ 2
walkedst ~ walked ~ 1
walkest ~ walk ~ 7
walkest orderly ~ *Gk* march in step
walketh ~ walks ~ 41
wanderest ~ wander ~ 1
wandereth ~ wanders ~ 6
want ~ lack, need
wanted ~ lacked, needed
wanteth ~ wants: lacks, needs
wanting ~ lacking, needing; i.e.
missing
wanton ~ sexually loose or
unrestrained; recklessly or
arrogantly ignoring justice,

decency, morality, etc.; un-
disciplined, unmanageable
wantonness ~ *Gk* unbridled lust,
licentiousness, lasciviousness,
shamelessness
wants ~ lacks, needs
ward ~ guard, custody, watch;
custody, guardianship,
confinement; *Arc* garrison,
guard, watch
ward ~ guard house, jail, prison
wards ~ *Arc* watches i.e. shifts
ware ~ wore
ware ~ *Arc* of aware: cautious
ware ~ wares, goods, merchandise
wares ~ goods, merchandise
warmeth ~ warms ~ 2
warp ~ weaving term: the threads
running lengthwise in the
loom and crossed by the weft
or woof
warreth ~ wars ~ 1
was set ~ i.e. had sat
was forward ~ *Gk* endeavored, gave
diligence, made haste
washest ~ wash
wast ~ were ~ 66
waste ~ wild; ruined
waste ~ destroy; wear out; ruin,
devastate
wasted ~ devastated, ruined
wastes ~ ruins, destroyed places
wasteth ~ wastes: ruins, devastates,
destroys
wasting ~ devastation, ruin
watcheth ~ watches ~ 3
watchings ~ vigils, sleepless
watchings
wateredst ~ watered ~ 1
waterest ~ water ~ 2
watereth ~ waters ~ 5
wavereth ~ wavers ~ 1

wax ~ grow, become

waxed ~ grew, became; grown, become

waxen ~ grown, become

waxeth ~ waxes: grows, becomes

waxing ~ growing, becoming

wayfaring ~ traveling, wandering

waymarks ~ road markers

ways ~ roads, paths

weakeneth ~ weakens ~ 2

wealth ~ *Obs* well-being; prosperity

weareth ~ wears ~ 1

wearieth ~ wearies ~ 2

weavest ~ weave ~ 1

weepest ~ weep ~ 3

weepeth ~ weeps ~ 4

weigheth ~ weighs ~ 2

welfare ~ well-being

wench ~ girl, maid-servant, young woman

went about ~ went or walked around

went a whoring ~ prostituted themselves: lit. through cult prostitution to false gods or fig. By spiritual unfaithfulness to the true God

wentest ~ went ~ 14

wert ~ were ~ 6

what thing soever ~ whatever thing

what supplication soever ~ whatever supplication

what saddle soever ~ whatever saddle

what prayer and supplication soever ~ whatever prayer and supplication

what place soever ~ whatever place

what things soever ~ whatever things

what wilt thou ~ will you (have): i.e. what do you want

what man soever ~ whatever man

what cause soever ~ whatever cause

what ~ who

what do ye ~ what are you (pl) doing?

whatsoever ~ whatever

wheaten ~ wheat

whelp ~ cub

whelps ~ cubs

whence ~ (from) where, (from) what place; where

whensoever ~ whenever (emphatic)

whereabout ~ *Obs* on which, about which

whereas ~ i.e. on the contrary, on the other hand; i.e. while; i.e. although, in reality

whereby ~ by which; *Arc* by what? How?

wherefore ~ therefore; for which cause, for this cause; *Arc* why?

wherein ~ in which; i.e. (in those things) in which; *Arc* how? In what way?

whereinsoever ~ *Obs* in whatever (way)

whereinto ~ into which whereinto ~ where to ~ into which ~ 3-

whereof ~ of what, which, whom; (something) of which

whereon ~ on which; *Arc* on what?

wheresoever ~ wherever (emphatic); at, in, or to whatever place

whereto ~ to which; to what?

whereunto ~ *Arc* of whereto: toward what end or direction; unto which; unto what?

whereupon ~ upon which, upon what; at which, because of which

wherewith ~ with which; that with which; *Arc* with what?

wherewithal ~ *Arc* of wherewith--*Arc* with what?

whet ~ sharpen, hone
whether ~ *Obs* if; whether or not; *Arc* which (of two)?
whiles ~ *Obs* while
whilst ~ *Obs* while
whirleth ~ whirls ~ 1
whisperer ~ slanderer, backbiter
whit ~ bit (small amount)
white ~ whiten
whited ~ whitewashed
whither ~ where, to what place
whithersoever ~ *Arc* of wheresoever: wherever (emphatic): to whatever place
whole ~ healthy. in health
wholly ~ completely, entirely
whomsoever ~ whomever (emphatic)
whore ~ prostitute, harlot; female engaging in promiscuous sexual intercourse: slut
whoredom ~ prostitution, fornication; fig. Being false to God, idolatry
whoremonger ~ man who has sexual intercourse with or associates with whores; fornicator, lecher (*Gk* male prostitute; fornicator)
whoremongers ~ men who have sexual intercourse with or associate with whores; fornicators, lechers (*Gk* male prostitutes; fornicators)
whores ~ prostitutes, harlots; promiscuous females, sluts
whoring ~ prostituted themselves (there): lit. through cult prostitution to false gods or fig. by spiritual unfaith-fulness to the true God
whorish ~ whore-like, lewd
whose soever ~ whoevers'

whose sign was ~ marked by the image of
whoso ~ *Arc* whoever (short for whosoever)
whosoever ~ whoever (emphatic)
wicked ~ wicked (one)
wiles ~ sly tricks; clever schemes
wilily ~ slyly, craftily, deceitfully
will ~ wish, want; *Gk* will to
willeth ~ wills ~ 1
wilt thou ~ i.e. do you want or wish
wilt ~ will, wish
wimples ~ folded garments worn by women to cover the head and neck (*Heb* cloaks)
winebibber ~ drunkard, wino
winebibbers ~ drunkards, winos
winefat ~ *Arc* wine vat, wine press
winketh ~ winks ~ 2
winneth ~ wins ~ 1
winnoweth ~ winnows ~ 1
winnoweth ~ separates chaff from grain (by blowing wind or air)
winter ~ spend winter
wipeth ~ wipes ~ 2
wise ~ in this way
wist ~ *Arc* knew
wit ~ *Arc* know or learn
wit ~ know ~ 3-
with one accord ~ in agreement or harmony; with one mind; "one-mindedly"; *Gk* one-minded
with ~ *Gk* together with meanwhile
withal ~ *Arc* with; with it, with that, therewith; meanwhile
withdrawest ~ withdraw ~ 1
withdraweth ~ withdraws ~ 1
withereth ~ withers ~ 8
withes ~ pl of withe--tough, flexible twigs used for binding

withheldest ~ withheld ~ 1
withholden ~ withheld
withholdeth ~ restrains
withholdeth ~ withholds ~ 4
within ~ inside
within ~ kjv margin: among
without life ~ *Gk* lifeless
without ~ outside; out-of-doors; *Rare*
    beyond
withs ~ withes ~ 3
withstand ~ resist, oppose
withstood ~ resisted, opposed
witnesseth ~ witnesses ~ 2
wittingly ~ knowingly
woe worth ~ alas
womankind ~ women in general
wonder ~ sign, miracle
wonderful ~ wonderfully
wonders ~ signs, miracles
wont ~ accustomed
woof ~ weaving term: weft--the yarns
    carried by the shuttle back and
    forth across the warp in
    weaving
worketh ~ works: does; *Gk* works
    out, produces
worlds ~ *Gk* universe, ages
wormwood ~ bitter-oil yielding plant
worship ~ *Arc* honor, dignity,
    worthiness
worshippeth ~ worships ~ 6
worthies ~ persons of great worth
wot ~ *Arc* know
wotteth ~ wots: *Arc* knows
would have ~ *Gk* wanted to
would ~ willed, wished, wanted;
    wanted to, wished to
would ~ will or want; i.e. want or
    wish that; want to or wish to
would thou wert ~ wish you were
wouldest ~ wanted or wished
wouldest ~ would: will or wish

wound ~ wrapped
woundedst ~ wounded ~ 1
woundeth ~ wounds ~ 1
wreathen ~ coiled, entwined, twisted
    to form a wreath
wrest ~ twist; distort or change the
    true meaning, purpose, use,
    etc.; pervert
writest ~ write ~ 2
writeth ~ writes ~ 1
wrongeth ~ wrongs ~ 1
wroth ~ angry, wrathful, incensed
wrough ~ worked, fashioned; toiled
wrought ~ worked: i.e. boiled,
    bubbled
wroughtest ~ wrought: worked
ye ~ YOU (plural) ~ 3985-
yea ~ yes
yesternight ~ *Arc* last night, (on) the
    night before
yet ~ still
yieldeth ~ yields ~ 4
yokefellow ~ companion, partner,
    associate
yonder ~ over there; at or in that
    place; i.e. that
you ~ YOU (plural) ~ 2615-
you-ward ~ *Arc* toward YOU (plural)
    ~ 3
your ~ YOUR (plural) ~ 1776-
yours ~ YOURS (plural) ~ 12-
yourselves ~ YOURSELVES (plural)
    ~ 191
Zacharias ~ Zachariah ~ 11

Order Blank (p. 1)

Name:_____

Address:_____

City & State:_____Zip:_____

*Credit Card #:*_____*Expires:*_____

[ ] Send *Colossians & Philemon--Preaching Verse by Verse* by Pastor D. A. Waite ($12+$5 S&H) hardback, 240 pages.

[ ] Send *Philippians--Preaching Verse by Verse* by Pastor D. A. Waite ($10+$5 S&H) hardback, 176 pages.

[ ] Send *Making Marriage Melodious* by Pastor D. A. Waite ($7+$3 S&H), perfect bound, 112 pages.

[ ] Send *Ephesians--Preaching Verse by Verse* by Pastor D. A. Waite ($12+$5 S&H) hardback, 224 pages.

[ ] Send *Galatians--Preaching Verse By Verse* by Pastor D. A. Waite ($12+$5 S&H) hardback, 216 pages.

[ ] Send *First Peter--Preaching Verse By Verse* by Pastor D. A. Waite ($10+$5 S&H) hardback, 176 pages.

[ ] Send *Fundamentalist MIS-INFORMATION on Bible Versions* by Dr. Waite ($7+$3 S&H) perfect bound, 136 pages

[ ] Send *Holes in the Holman Christian Standard Bible* by Dr. Waite ($3+$2 S&H) A printed booklet, 40 pages

[ ] Send *Central Seminary Refuted on Bible Versions* by Dr. Waite ($10+$3 S&H) A perfect bound book, 184 pages

[ ] Send *Fundamentalist Distortions on Bible Versions* by Dr. Waite ($6+$3 S&H) A perfect bound book, 80 pages

[ ] Send *Burgon's Warnings on Revision* by DAW ($7+$3 S&H) A perfect bound book, 120 pages in length.

[ ] Send *The Case for the King James Bible* by DAW ($7+$3 S&H) A perfect bound book, 112 pages in length.

[ ] Send *Foes of the King James Bible Refuted* by DAW ($10+$4 S&H) A perfect bound book, 164 pages in length.

[ ] Send *The Revision Revised* by Dean Burgon ($25 + $4 S&H) A hardback book, 640 pages in length.

Send or Call Orders to:
THE BIBLE FOR TODAY
900 Park Ave., Collingswood, NJ 08108
Phone: 856-854-4452; FAX:--2464; Orders: 1-800 JOHN 10:9
E-Mail Orders: BFT@BibleForToday.org; Credit Cards O K

Order Blank (p. 2)

Name:_____

Address:_____

City & State:_____Zip:_____

Credit Card #:_____Expires:_____

Other Materials on the KJB & T.R.

[ ] Send *The Last 12 Verses of Mark* by Dean Burgon ($15+$4 S&H) A hardback book 400 pages.

[ ] Send *The Traditional Text* hardback by Burgon ($16 + $4 S&H) A hardback book, 384 pages in length.

[ ] Send *Summary of Traditional Text* by Dr. Waite ($3 +$2)

[ ] Send *Summary of Causes of Corruption*, DAW ($3+$2)

[ ] Send *Causes of Corruption* by Burgon ($15 + $4 S&H) A hardback book, 360 pages in length.

[ ] Send *Inspiration and Interpretation*, Dean Burgon ($25+$4 S&H) A hardback book, 610 pages in length.

[ ] Send *Summary of Inspiration* by Dr. Waite ($3 + $2 S&H)

[ ]Send *Contemporary Eng. Version Exposed*, DAW ($3+$2)

[ ] Send *Westcott & Hort's Greek Text & Theory Refuted by Burgon's Revision Revised--Summarized* by Dr. D. A. Waite ($7.00 + $3 S&H), 120 pages, perfect bound.

[ ] Send *Defending the King James Bible* by Dr.Waite $13+$4 S&H) A hardback book, indexed with study questions.

[ ] Send *Guide to Textual Criticism* by Edward Miller ($7 +$4)

[ ] Send *Westcott's Denial of Resurrection*, Dr. Waite ($4+$3)

[ ] Send *Four Reasons for Defending KJB* by DAW ($3+$3)

[ ] Send *Vindicating Mark 16:9-20* by Dr. Waite ($3+$3 S&H)

[ ] Send *Dean Burgon's Confidence in KJB* by DAW ($3+$3)

[ ] Send *Readability of A.V. (KJB)* by D. A. Waite, Jr. ($6 +$3)

[ ] Send *NIV Inclusive Language Exposed* by DAW ($5+$3)

[ ] Send *26 Hours of KJB Seminar* (4 videos) by DAW ($50.00)

Send or Call Orders to:
THE BIBLE FOR TODAY
900 Park Ave., Collingswood, NJ 08108
Phone: 856-854-4452; FAX:--2464; Orders: 1-800 JOHN 10:9
E-Mail Orders: BFT@BibleForToday.org; Credit Cards OK

ained